William Sim
Colouring
The Lion City

A sophisticated activity book

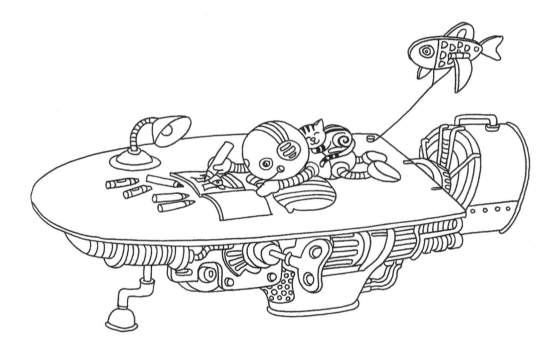

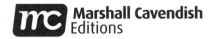

mc **Marshall Cavendish**
Editions

© 2015 Marshall Cavendish International (Asia) Private Limited
Reprinted 2015

This book published by
Marshall Cavendish Editions
An imprint of Marshall Cavendish International
1 New Industrial Road, Singapore 536196

The publisher makes no representation or warranties with respect to the contents of this book, and specifically
disclaims any implied warranties or merchantability or fitness for any particular purpose, and shall in no event
be liable for any loss of profit or any other commercial damage, including but not limited to special, incidental,
consequential, or other damages.

Other Marshall Cavendish Offices
Marshall Cavendish Corporation. 99 White Plains Road, Tarrytown NY 10591-9001, USA • Marshall
Cavendish International (Thailand) Co Ltd. 253 Asoke, 12th Flr, Sukhumvit 21 Road, Klongtoey Nua,
Wattana, Bangkok 10110, Thailand • Marshall Cavendish (Malaysia) Sdn Bhd, Times Subang, Lot 46,
Subang Hi-Tech Industrial Park, Batu Tiga, 40000 Shah Alam, Selangor Darul Ehsan, Malaysia

Marshall Cavendish is a trademark of Times Publishing Limited.

National Library Board, Singapore Cataloguing-in-Publication Data
Sim, William, artist.
Colouring the Lion City : a sophisticated activity book / William Sim. – Singapore :
Marshall Cavendish Editions, [2015]
pages cm
ISBN : 978-981-4677-94-3 (paperback)
1. Singapore – In art. 2. Coloring books. I. Title.
NC344.7.S553
741.95957 – dc23   OCN914218079

Printed in Singapore by Markono Print Media Pte Ltd

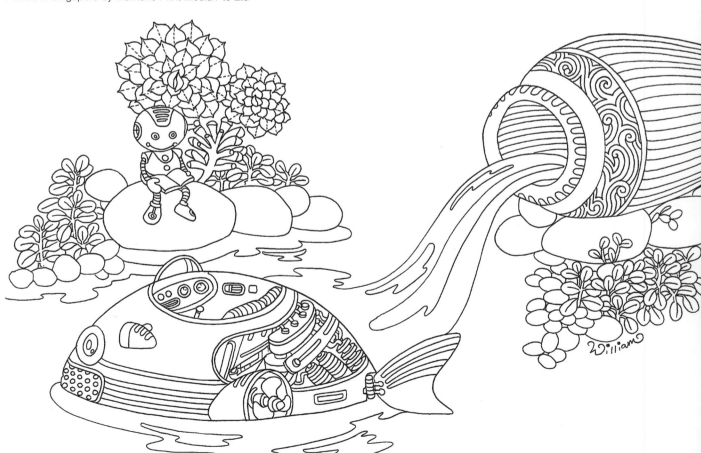

Welcome to the Lion City

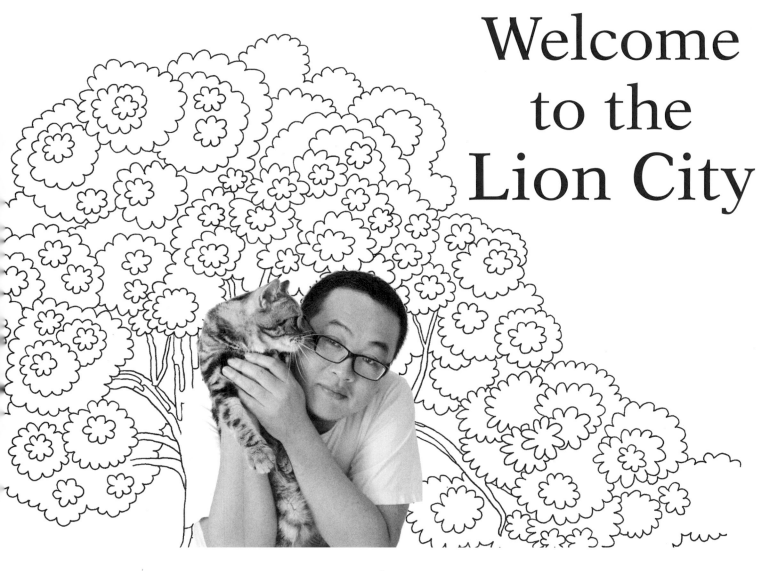

About the Author

William Sim's art often portrays a fantasy world in a kaleidoscope of candy hues and shades. The subjects, a blend of nature and mechanical objects, collaborate individually and collectively to depict dreamscapes of immense optimism. Branding himself as the Merchant of Happiness, William is a full-time art practitioner and a partner at a visual arts studio based in Singapore since 1997. He has showcased his paintings in various group and solo exhibitions in Singapore and countries like South Korea, Taiwan and Hong Kong.

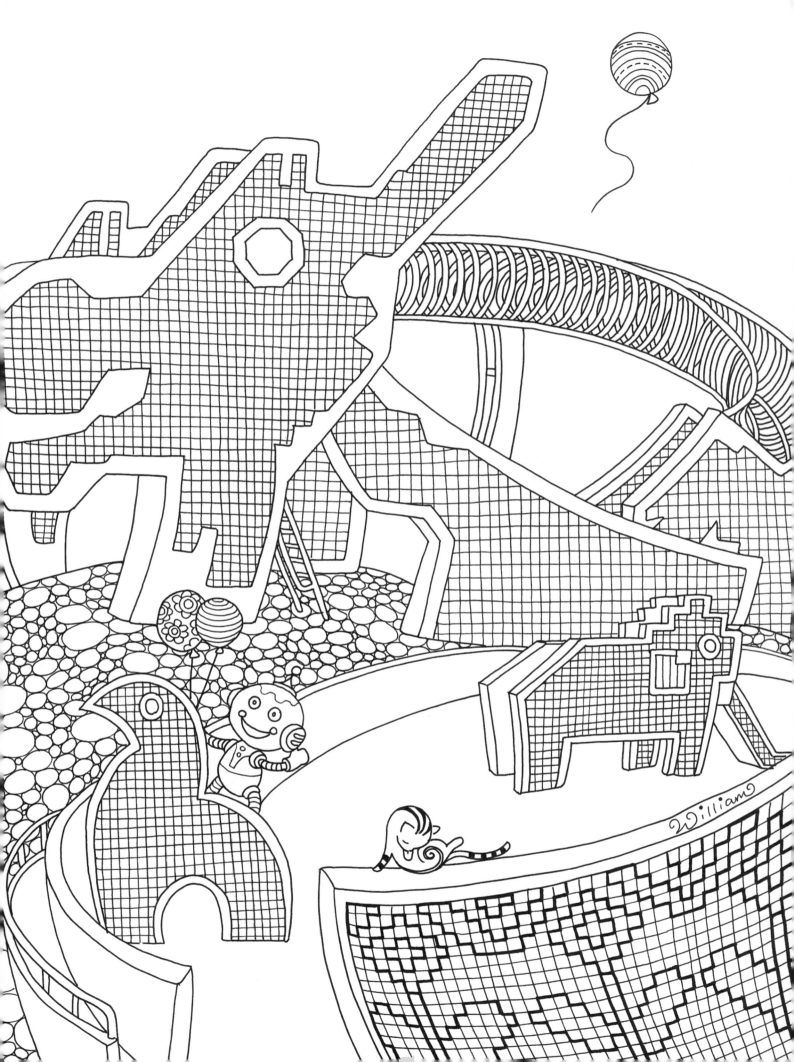

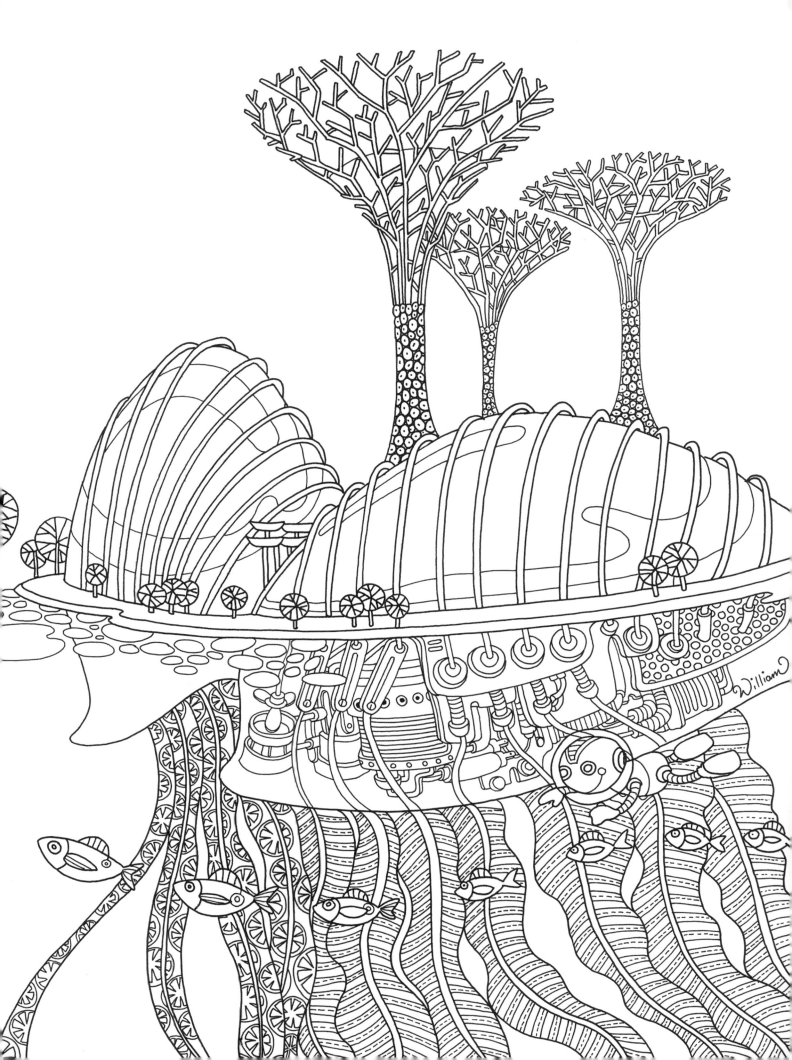

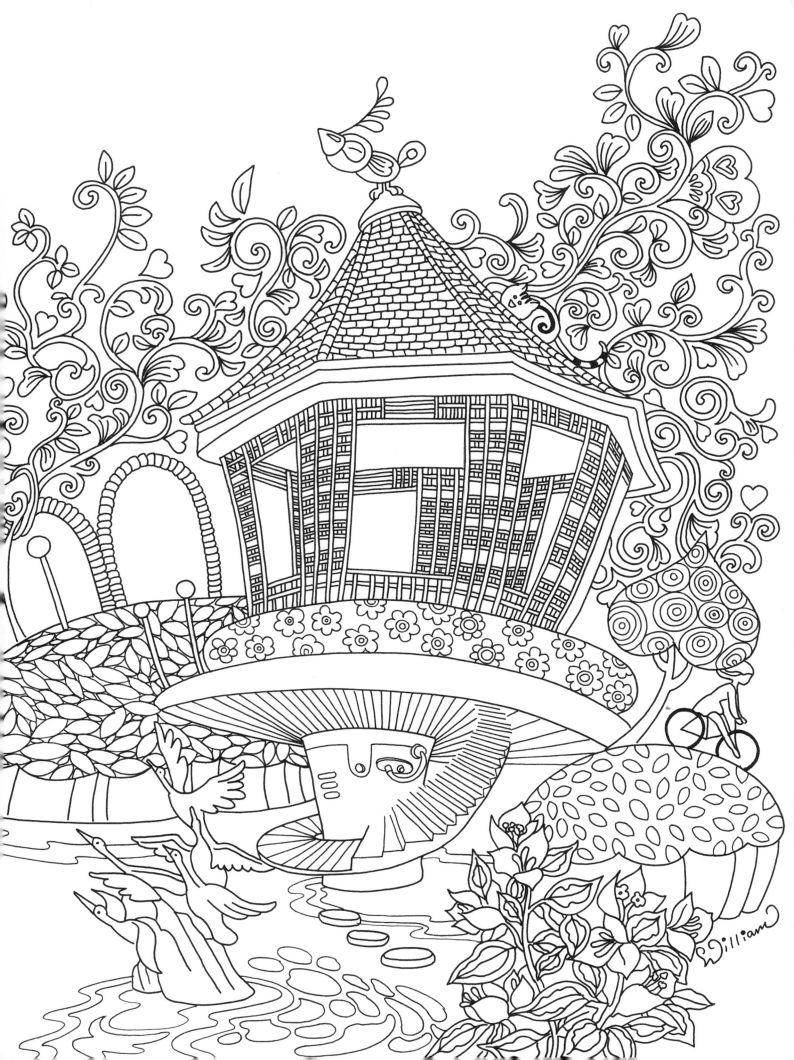

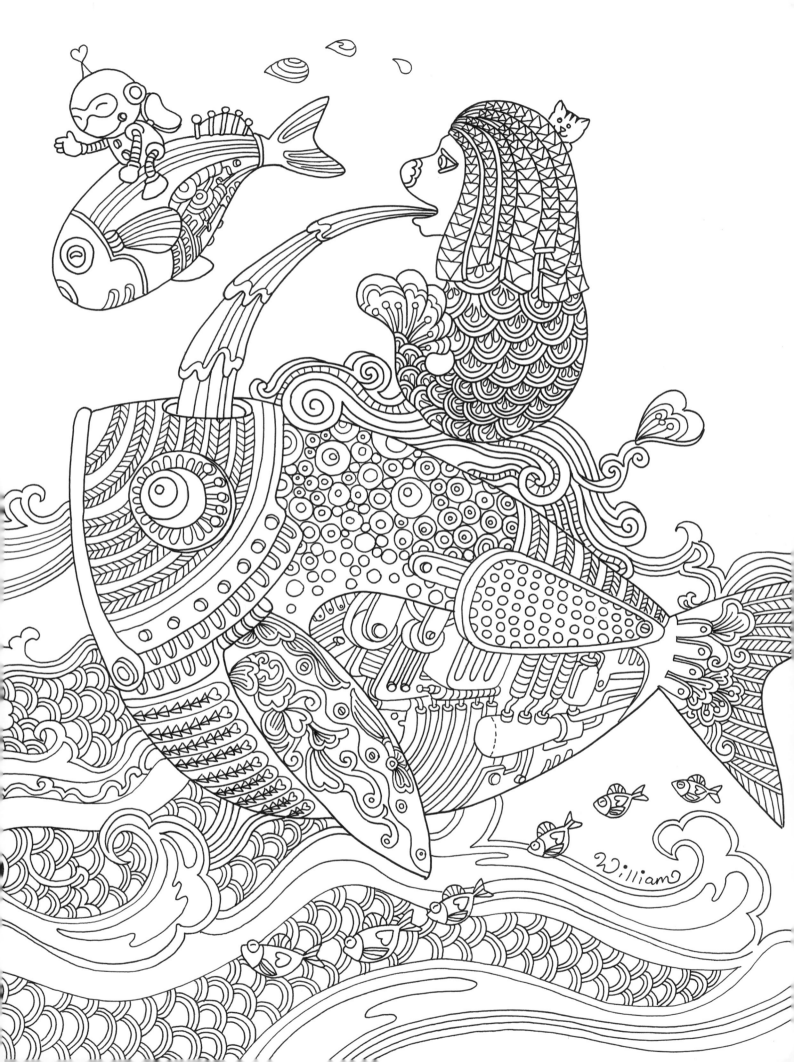

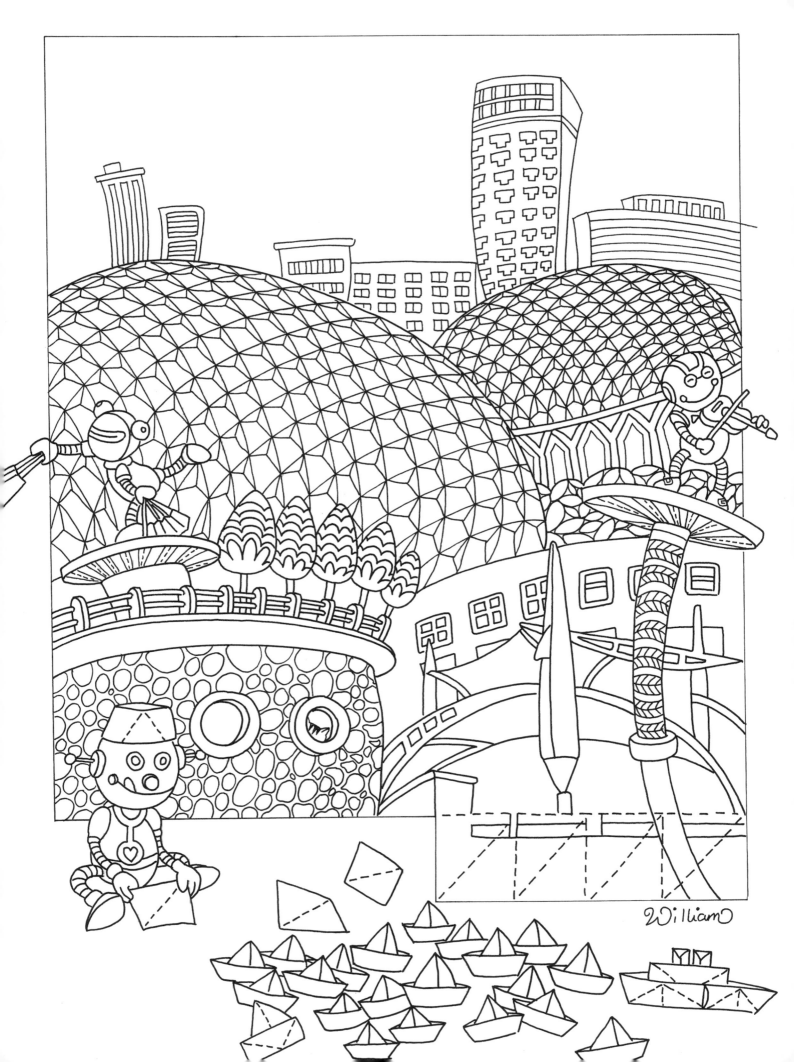

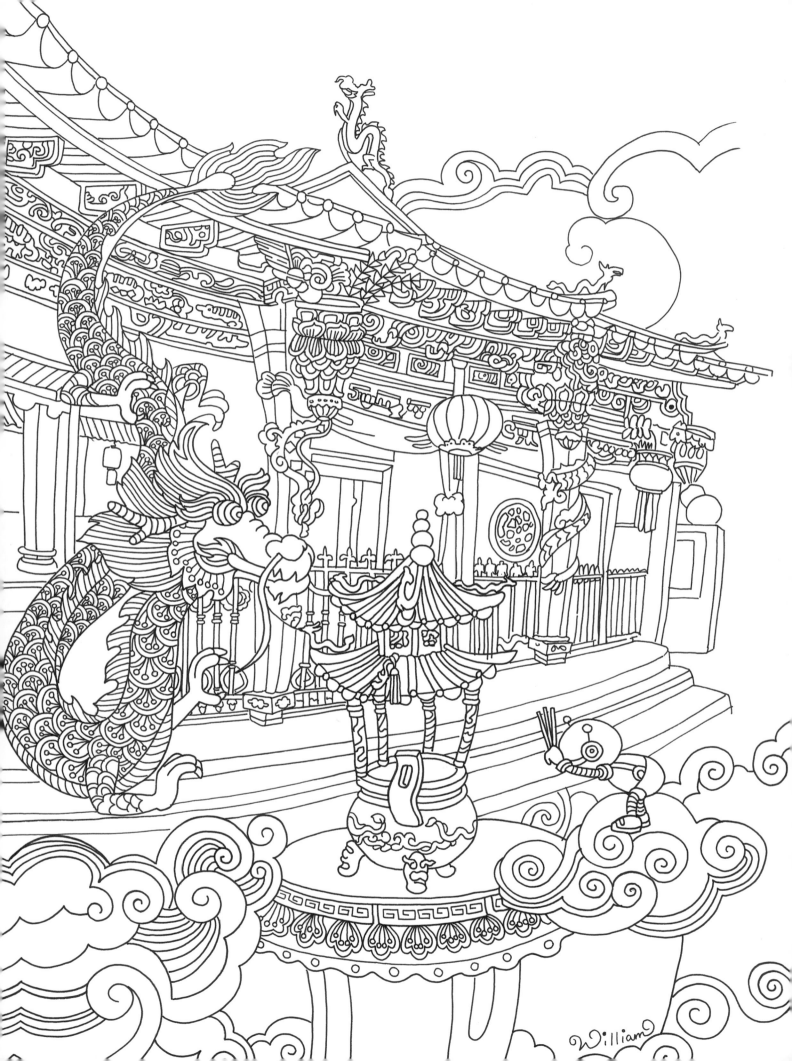

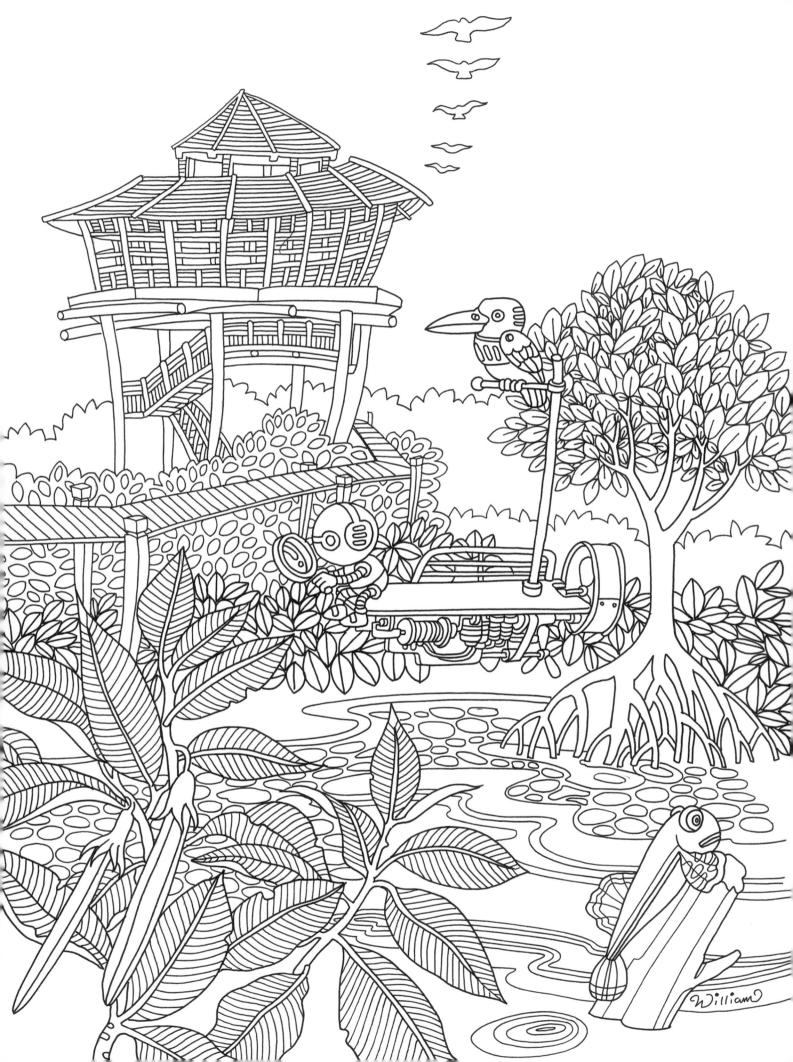

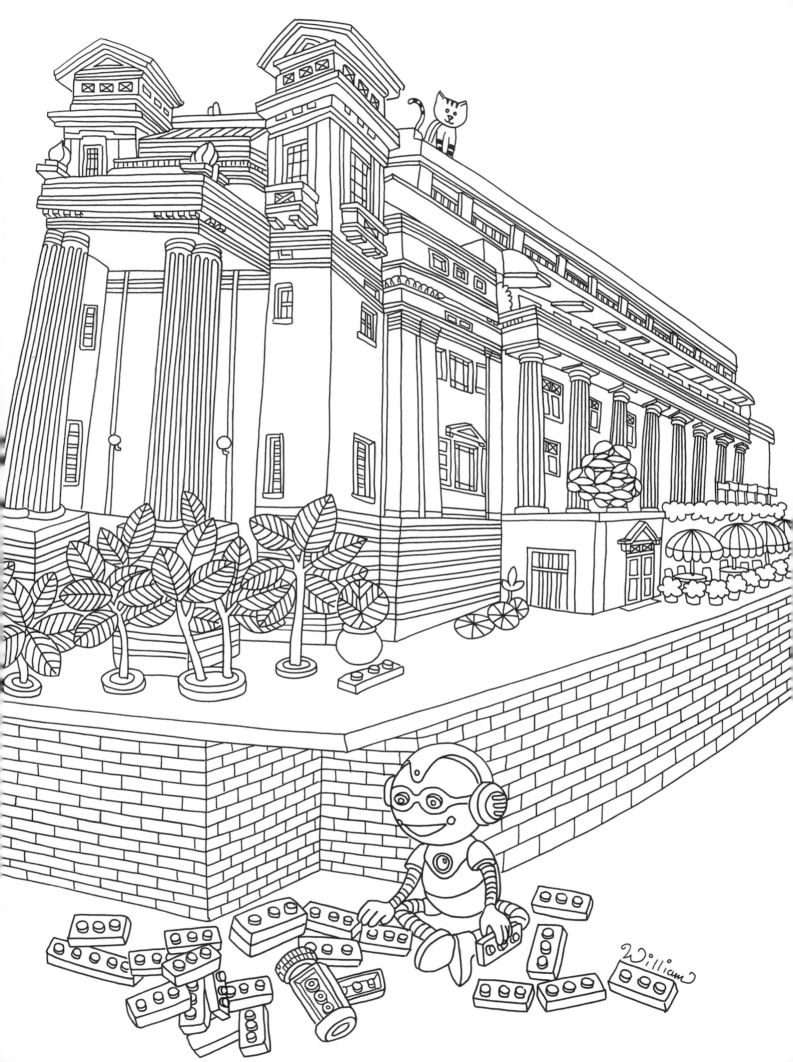

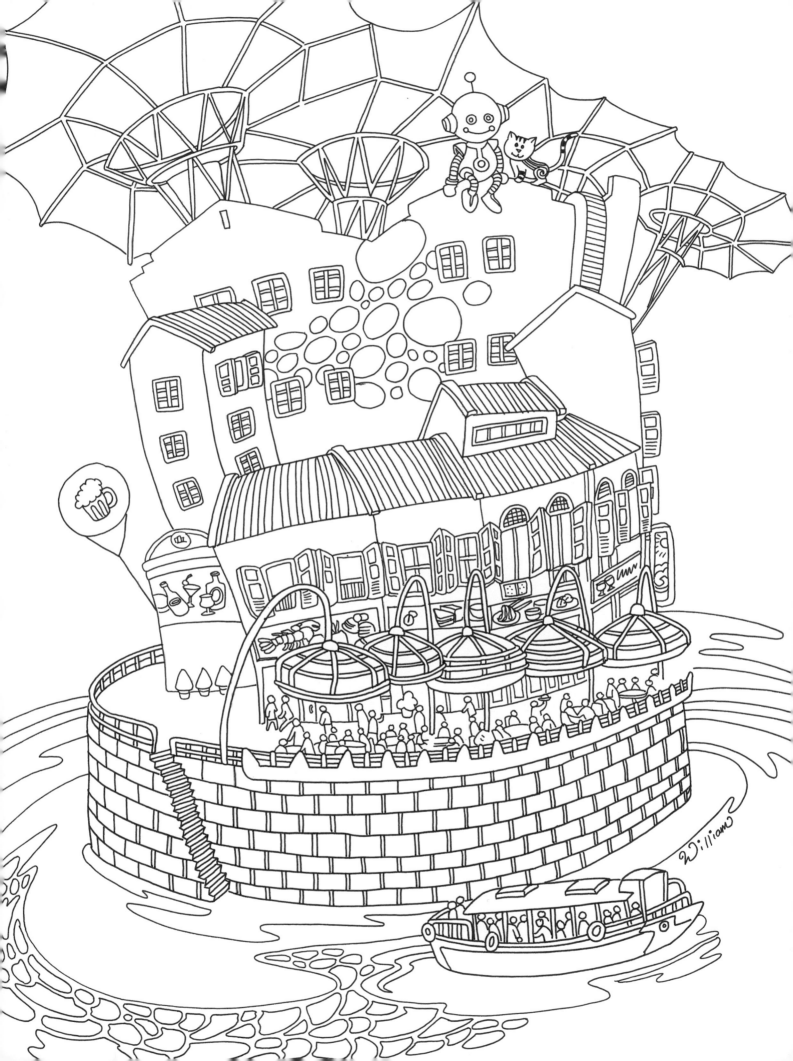

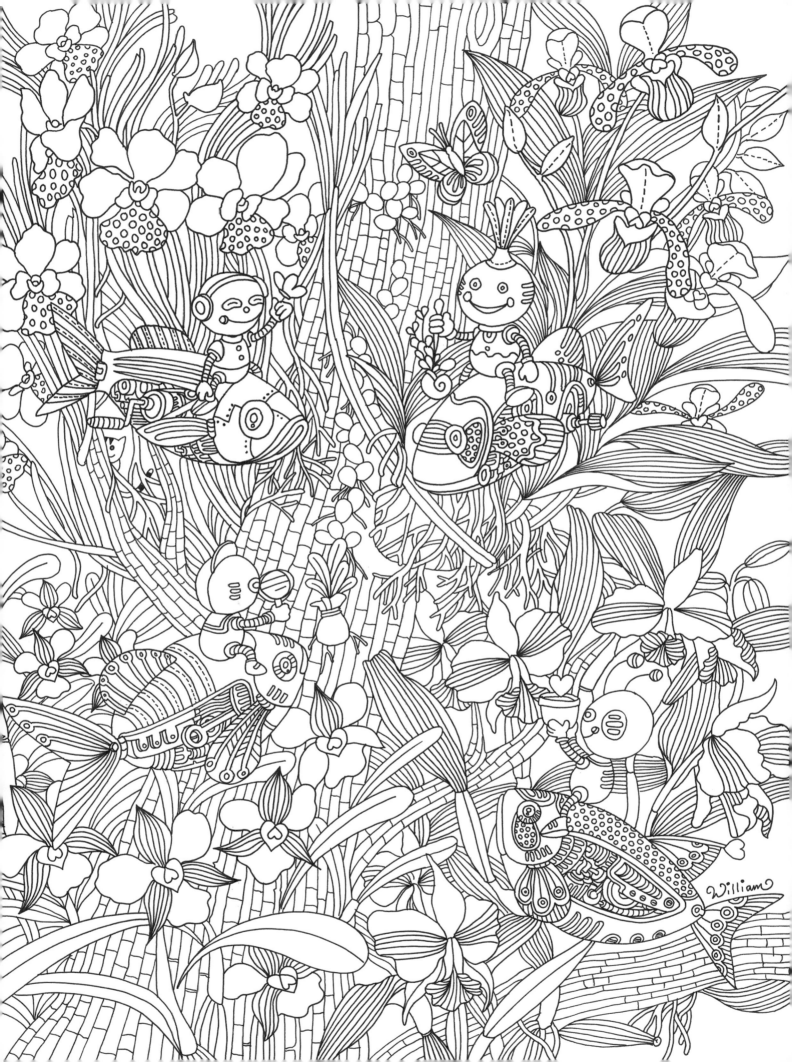

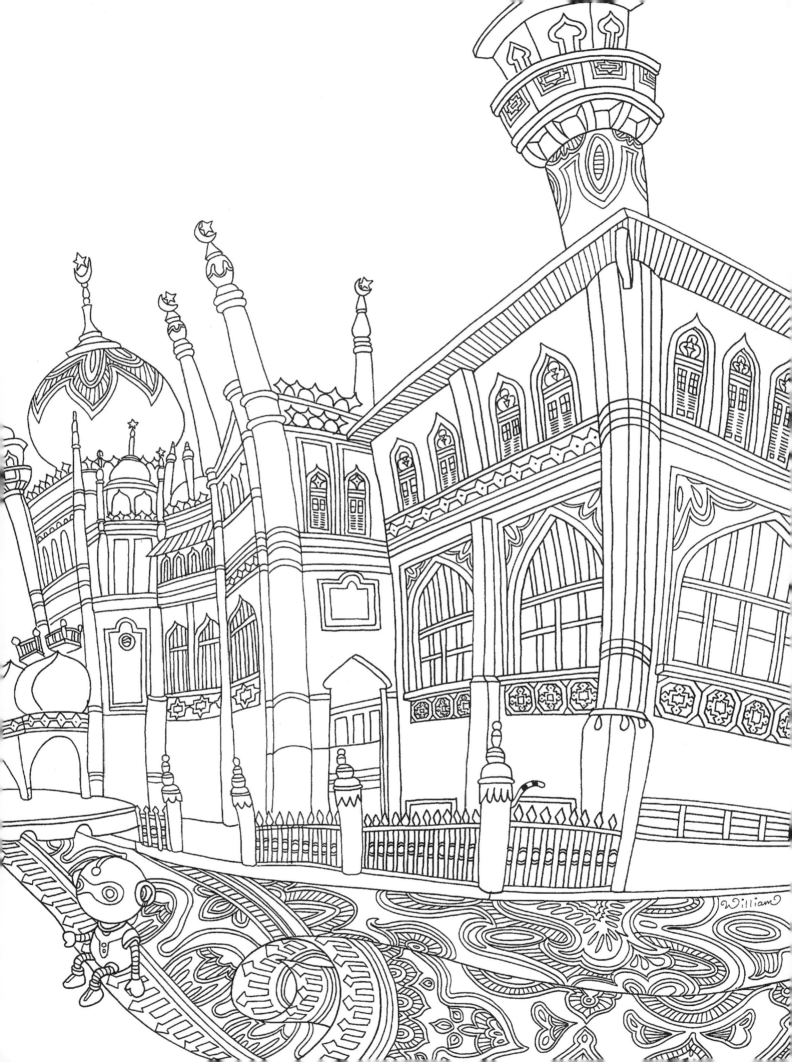

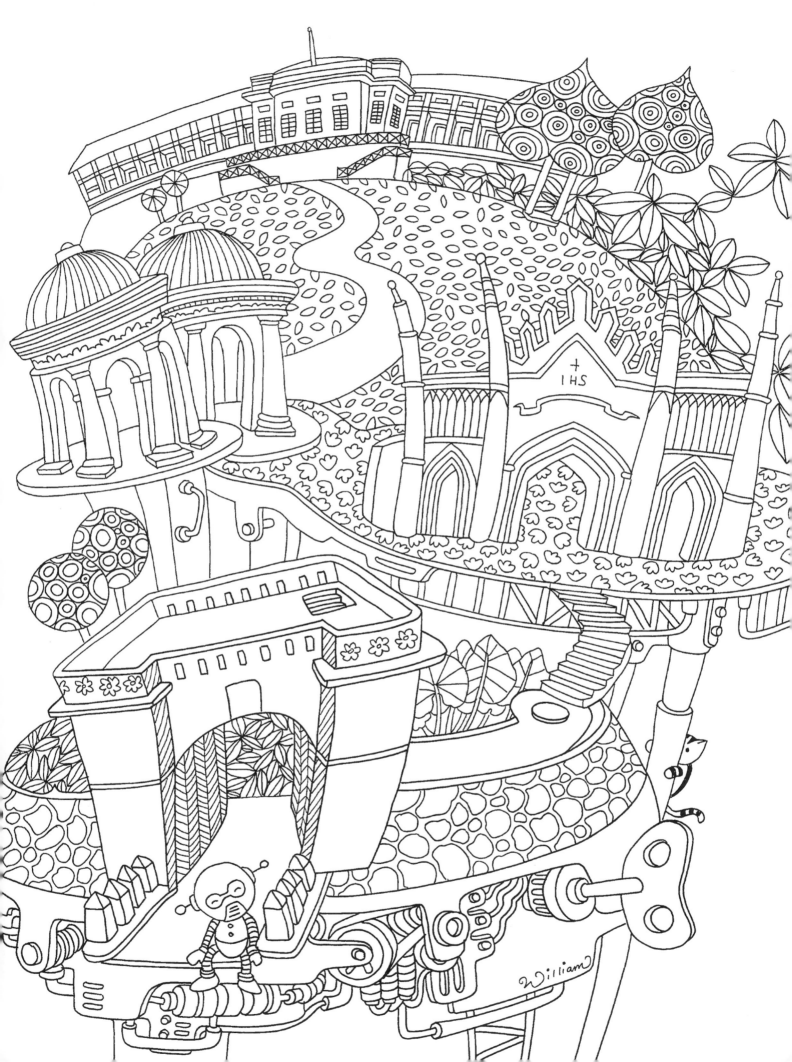

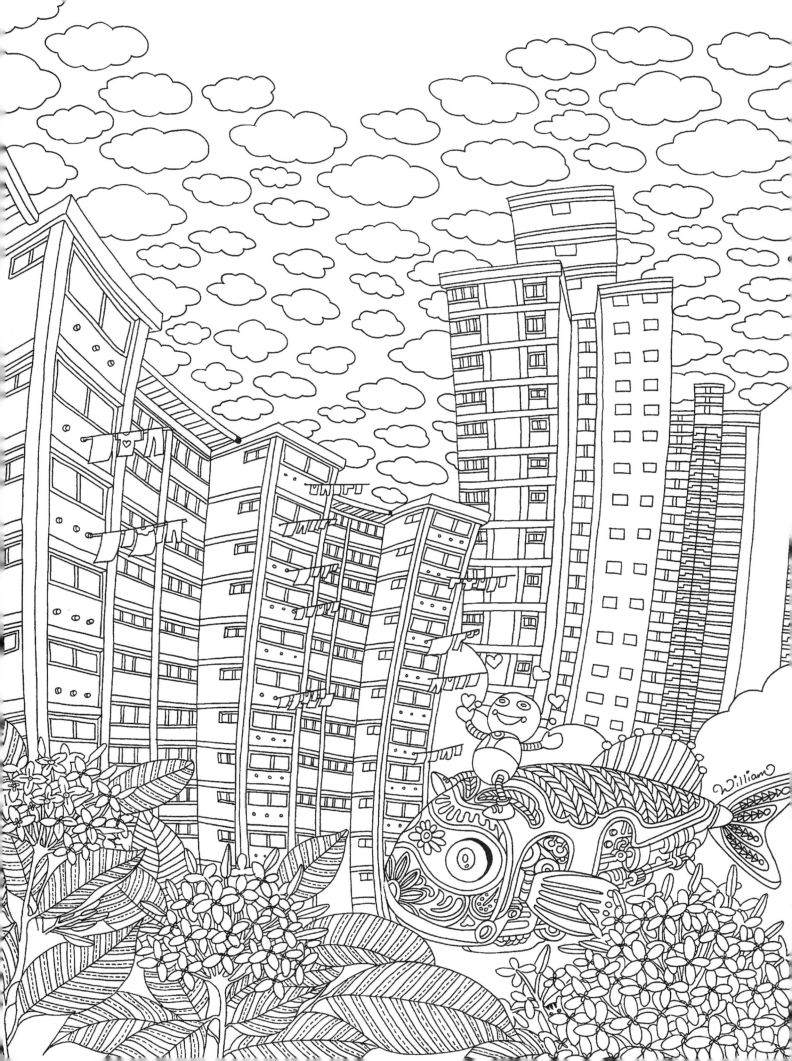

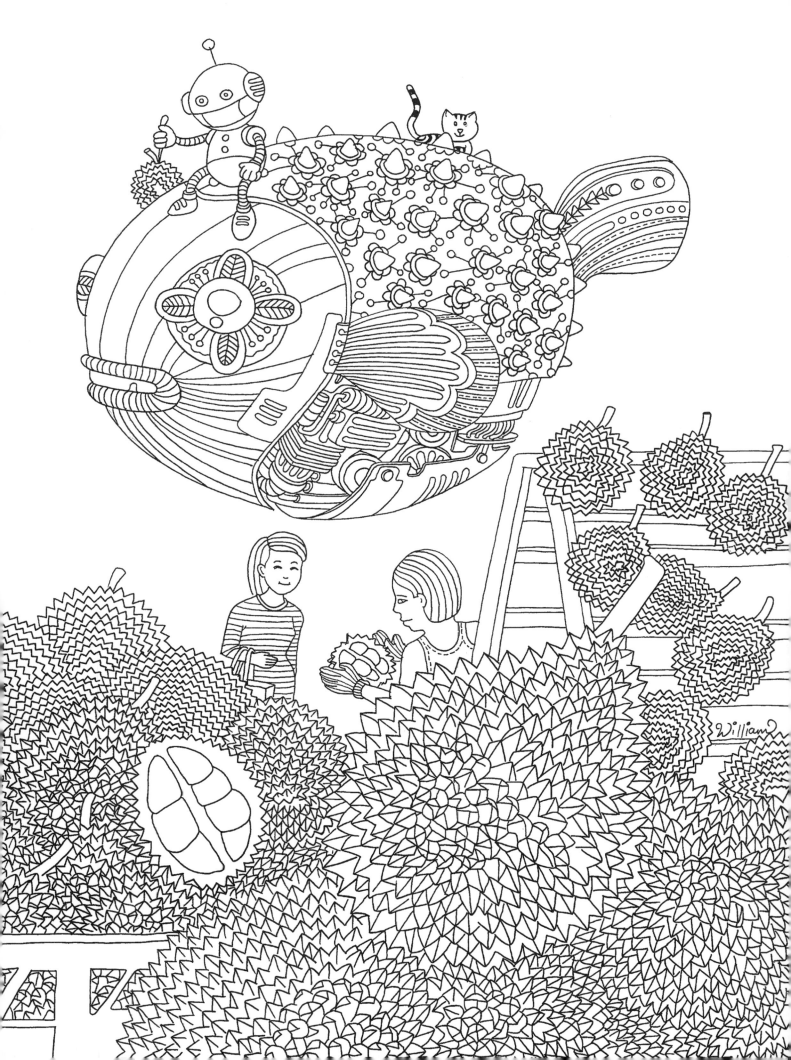

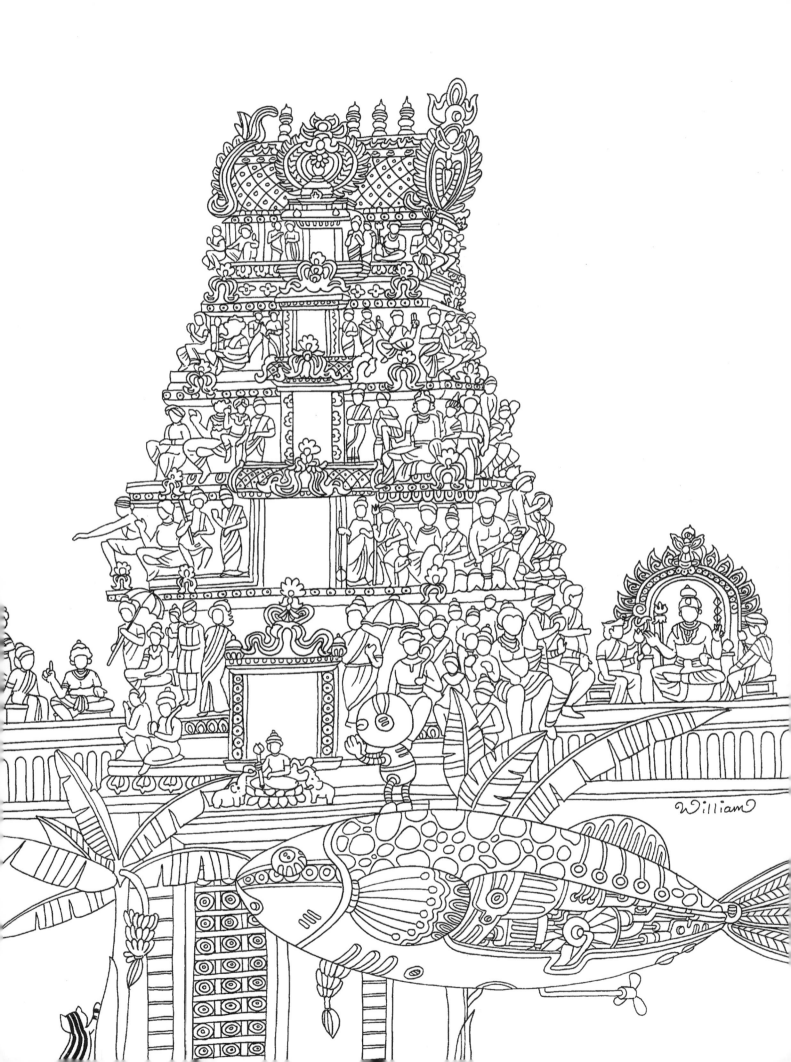

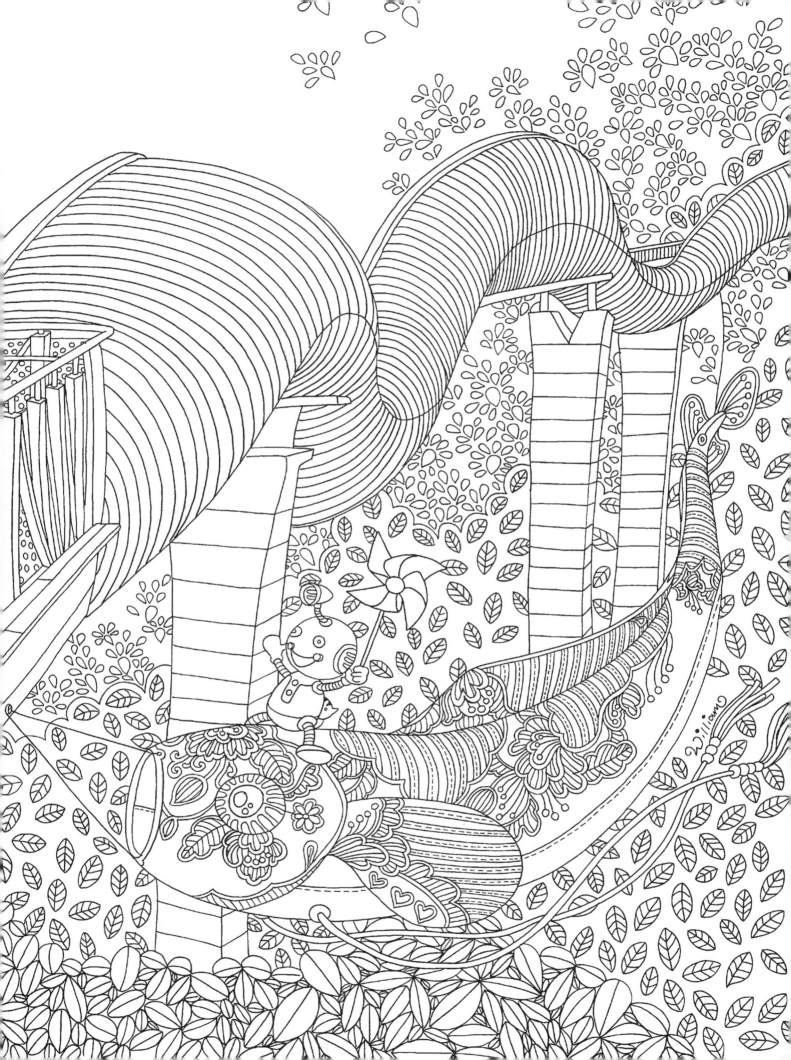

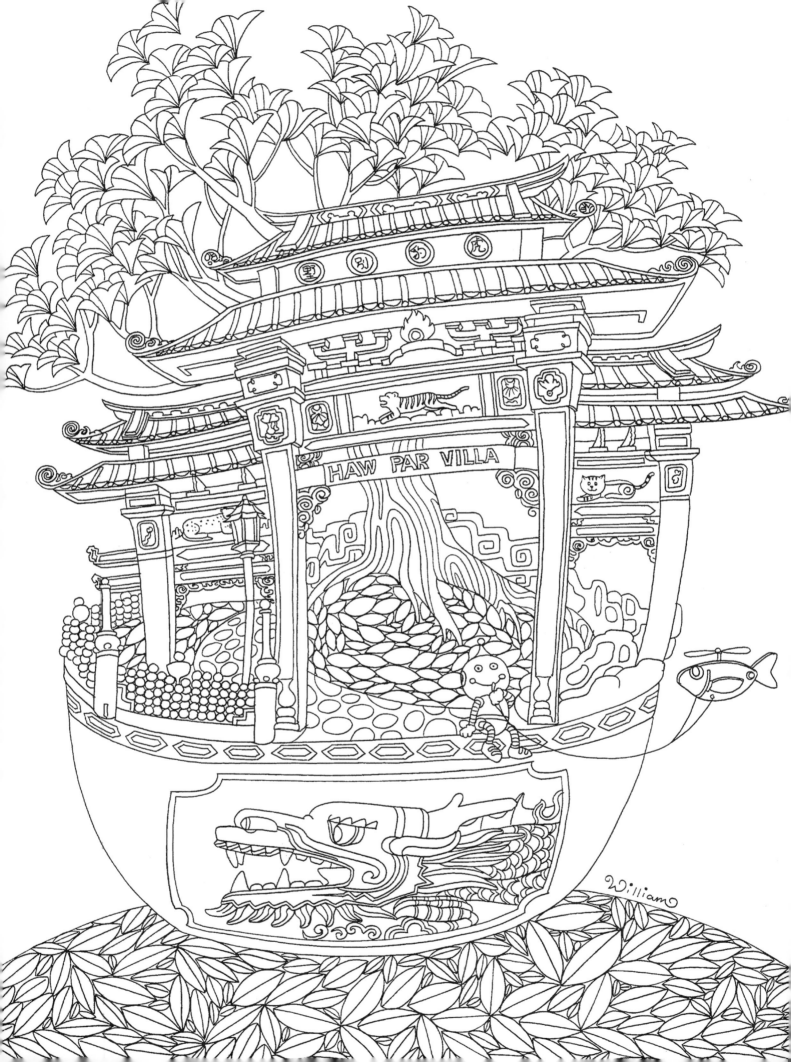

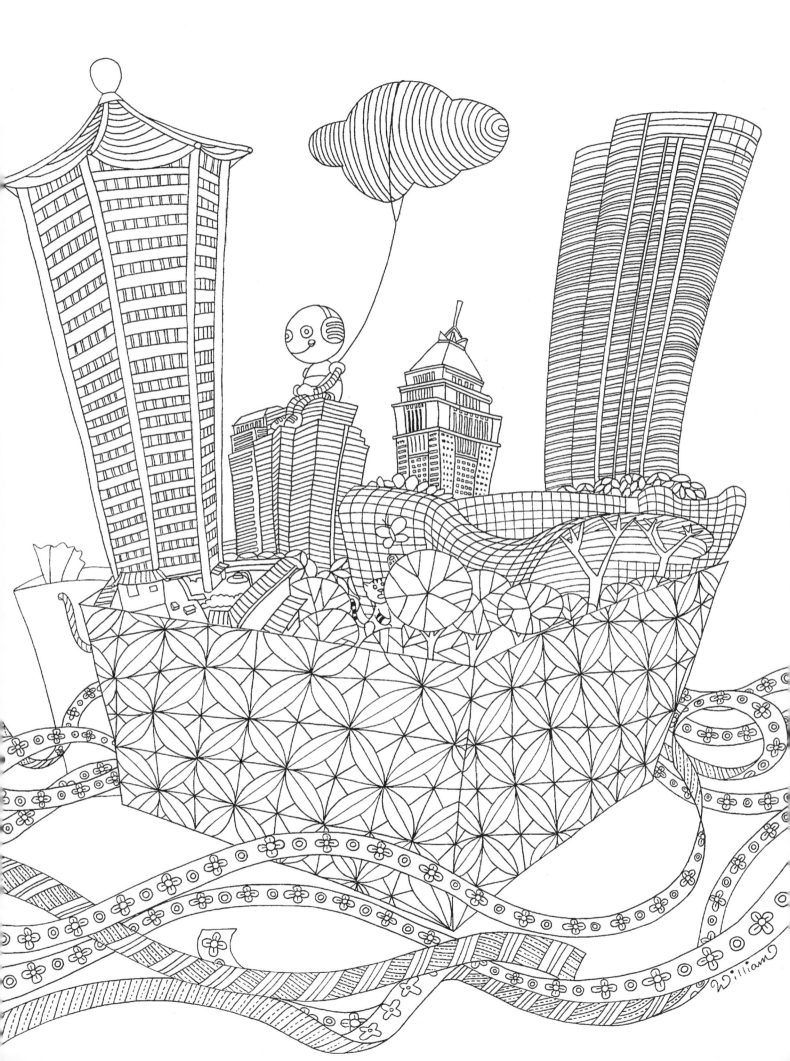

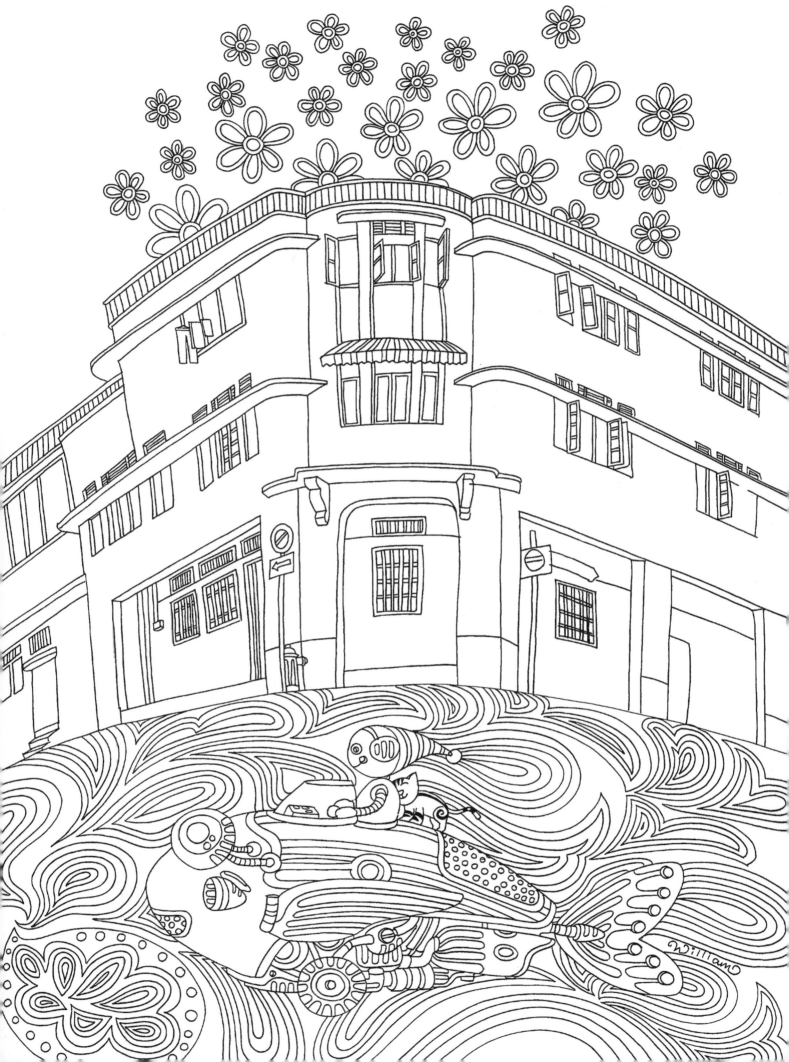

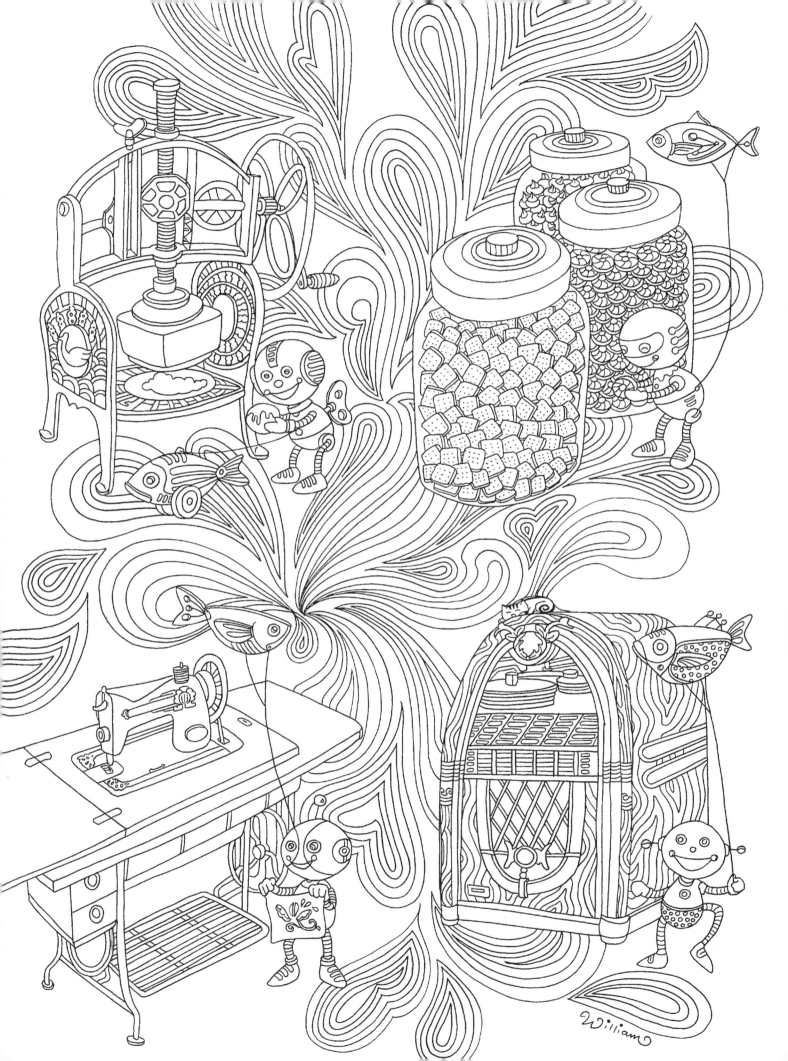

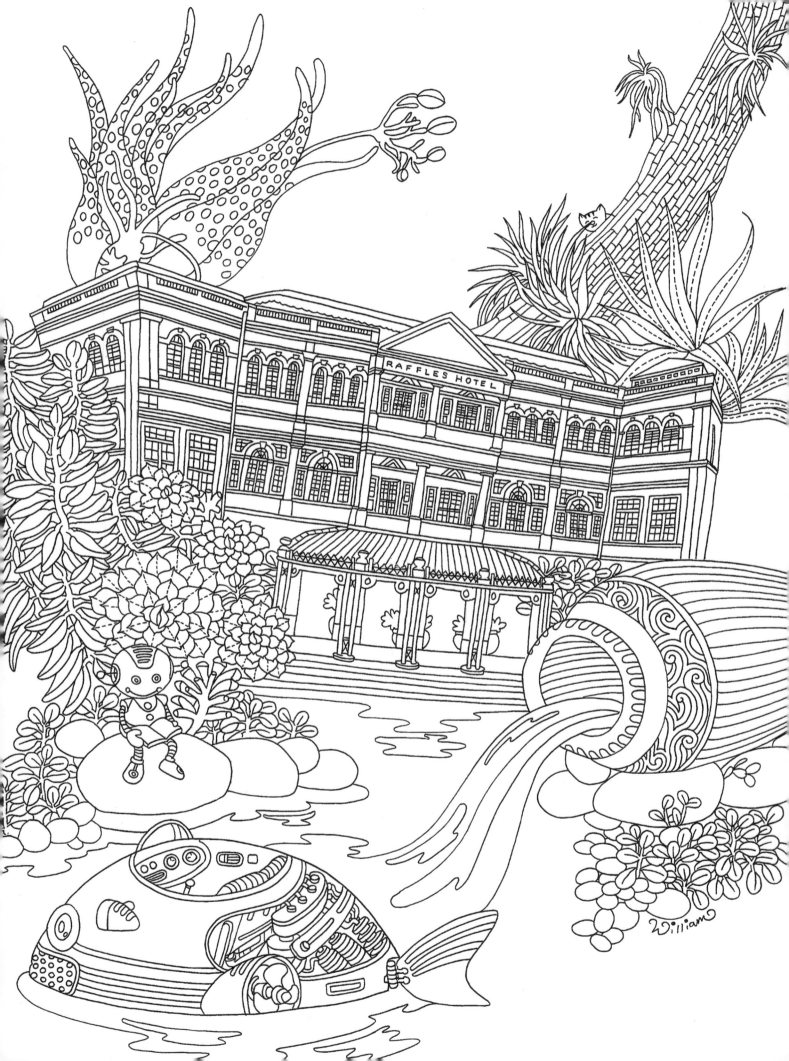

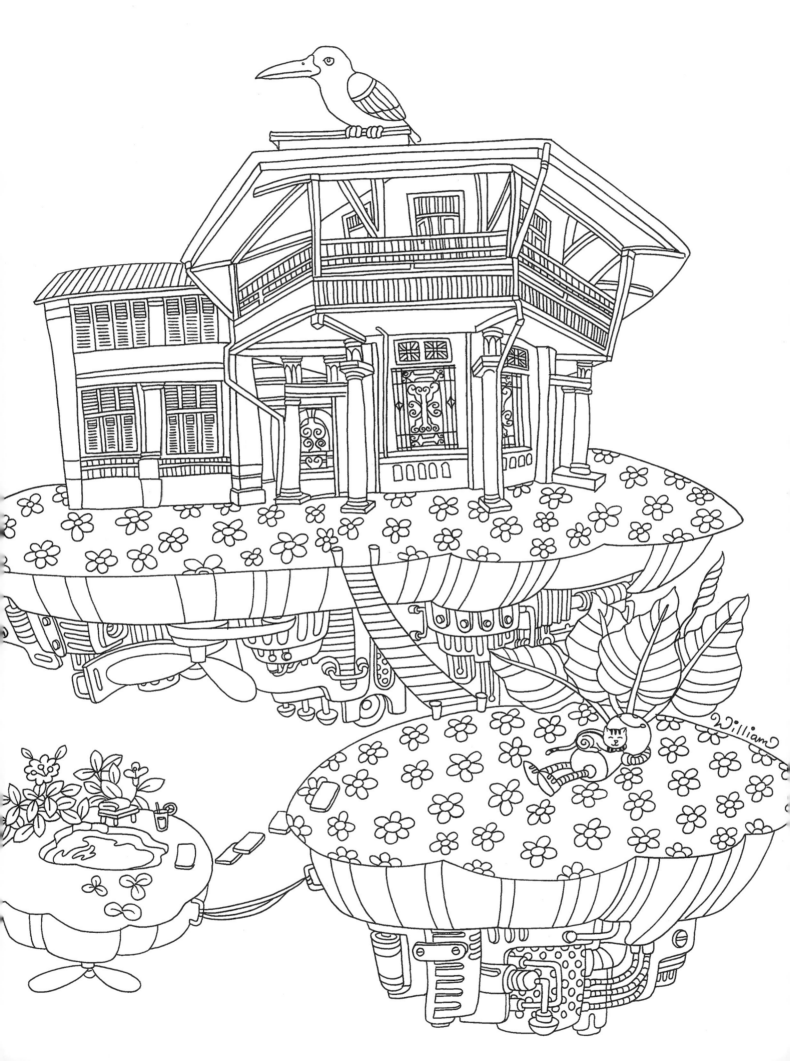

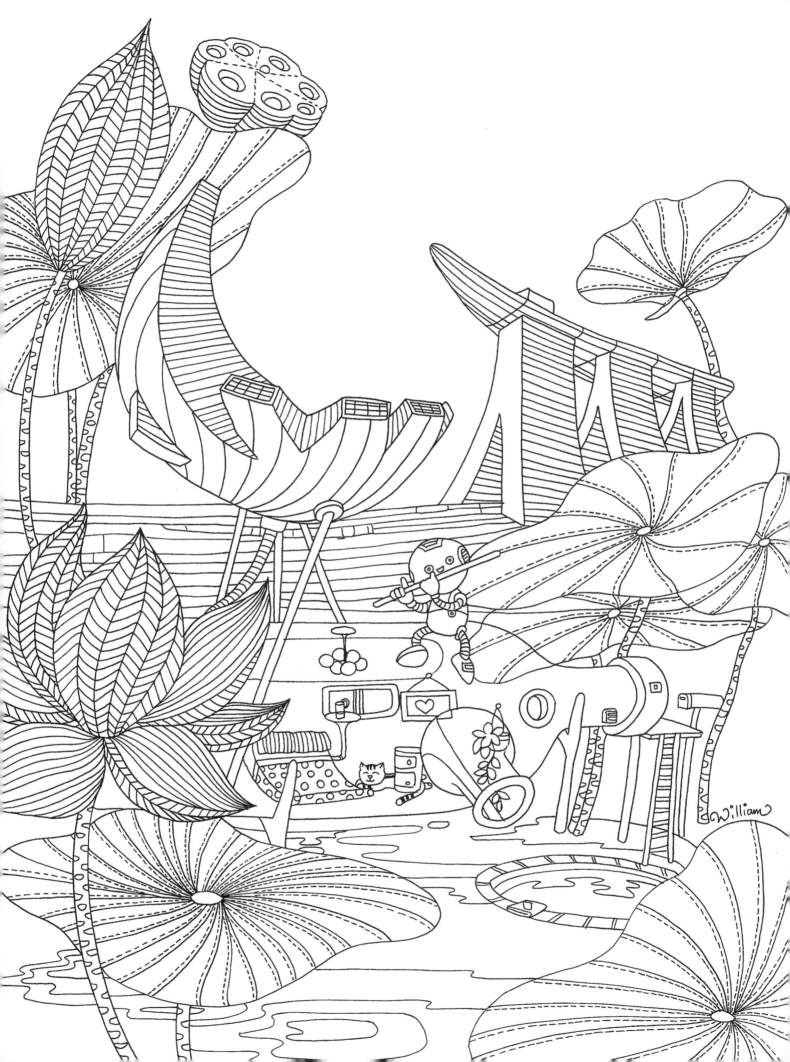

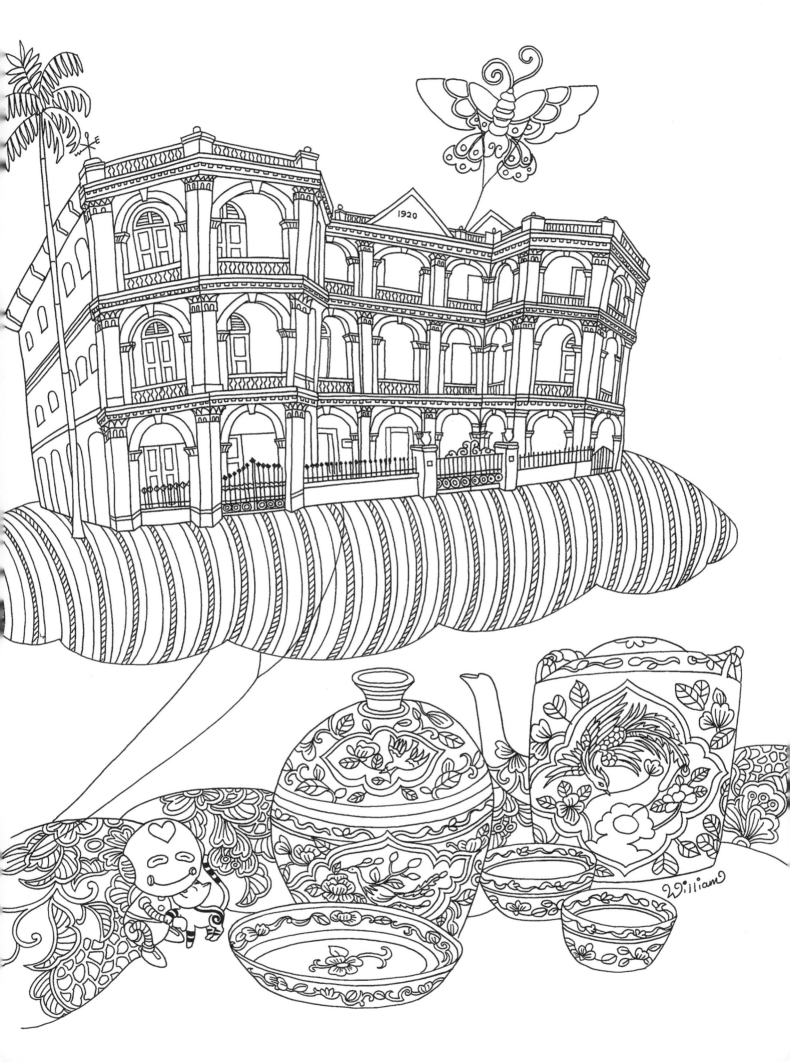

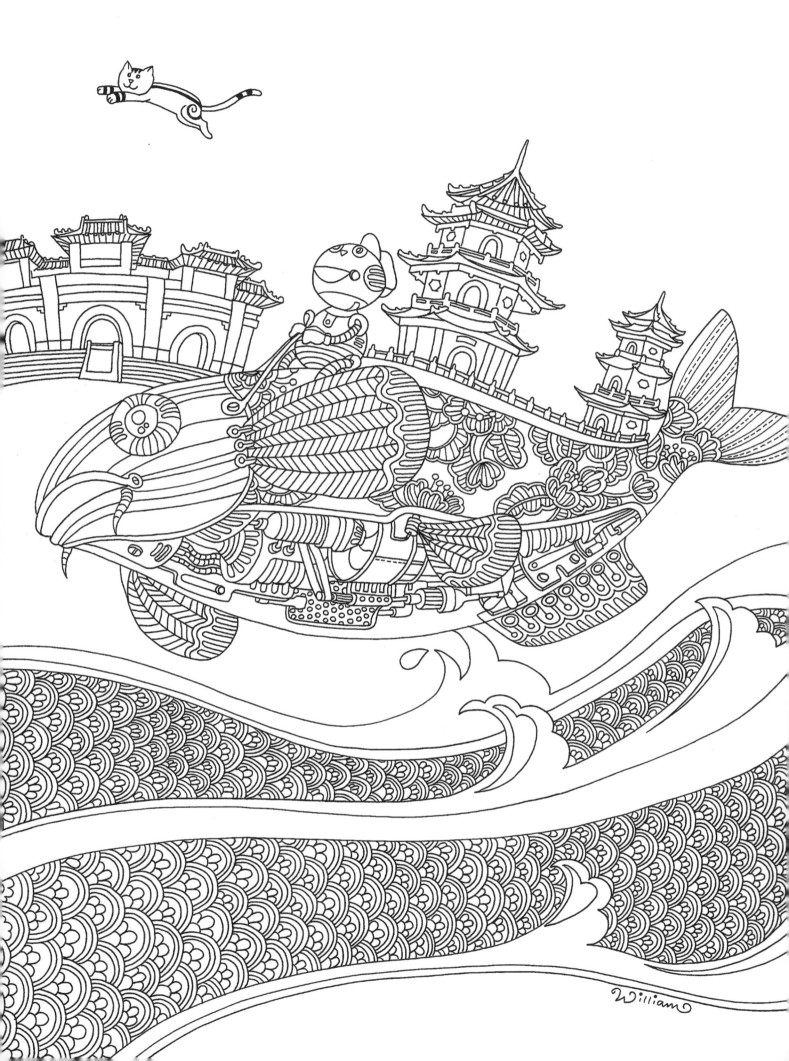

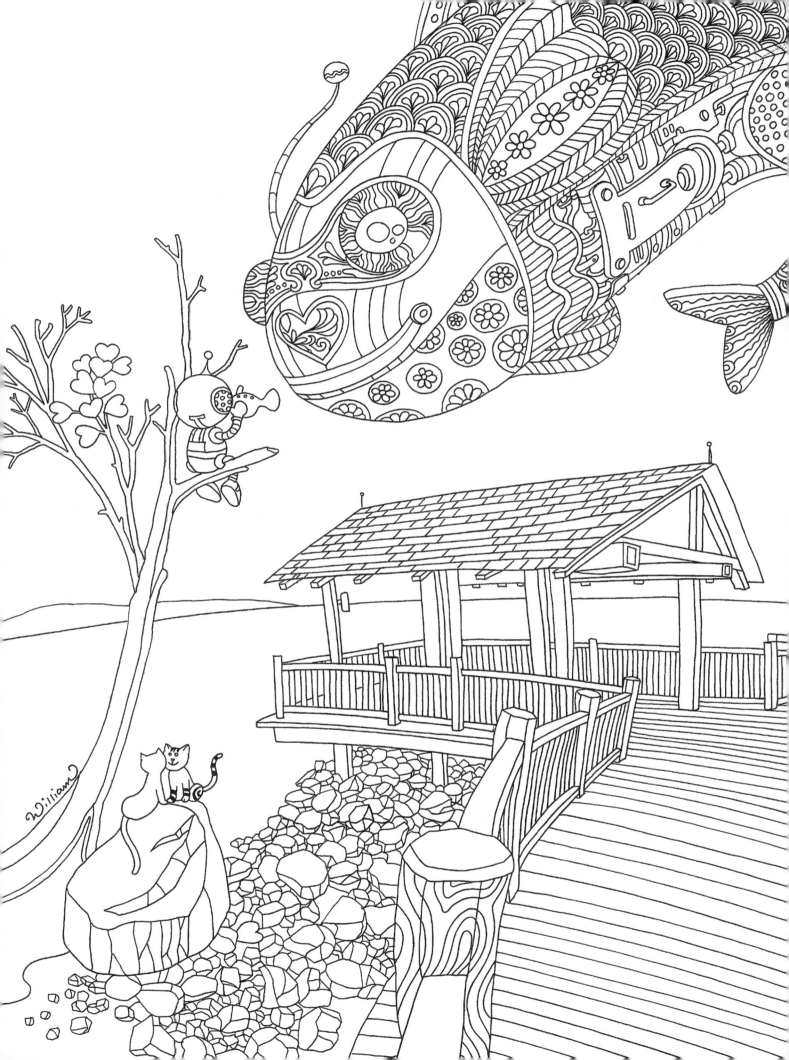

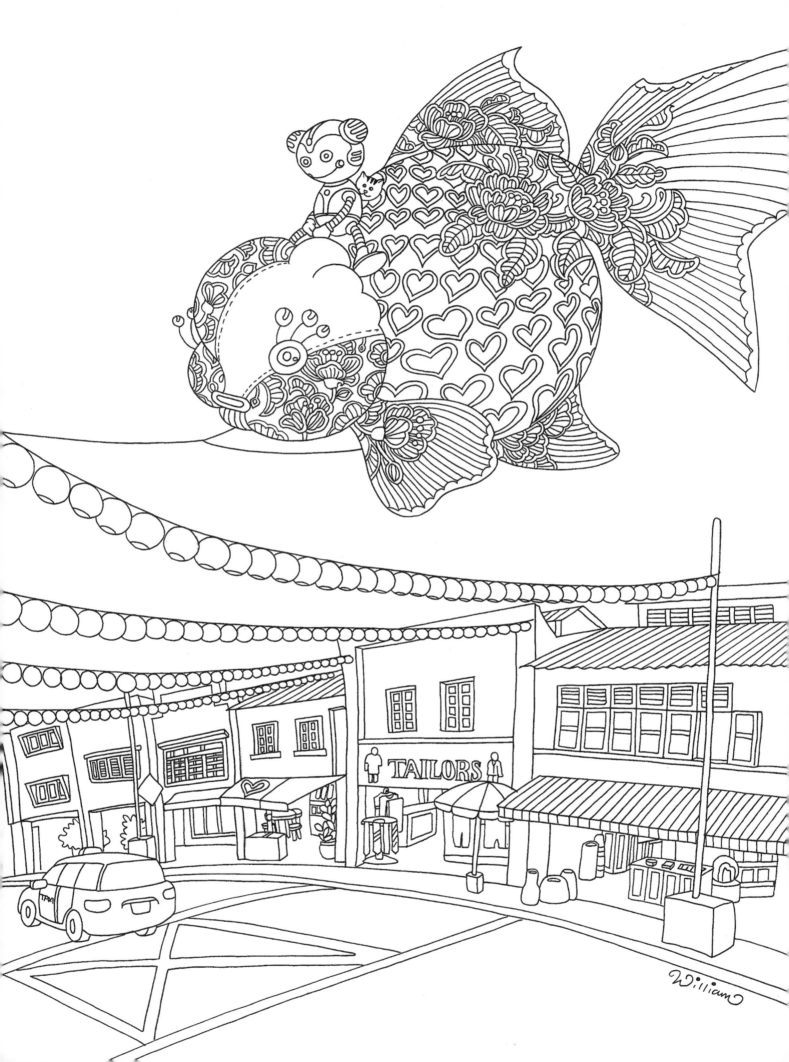

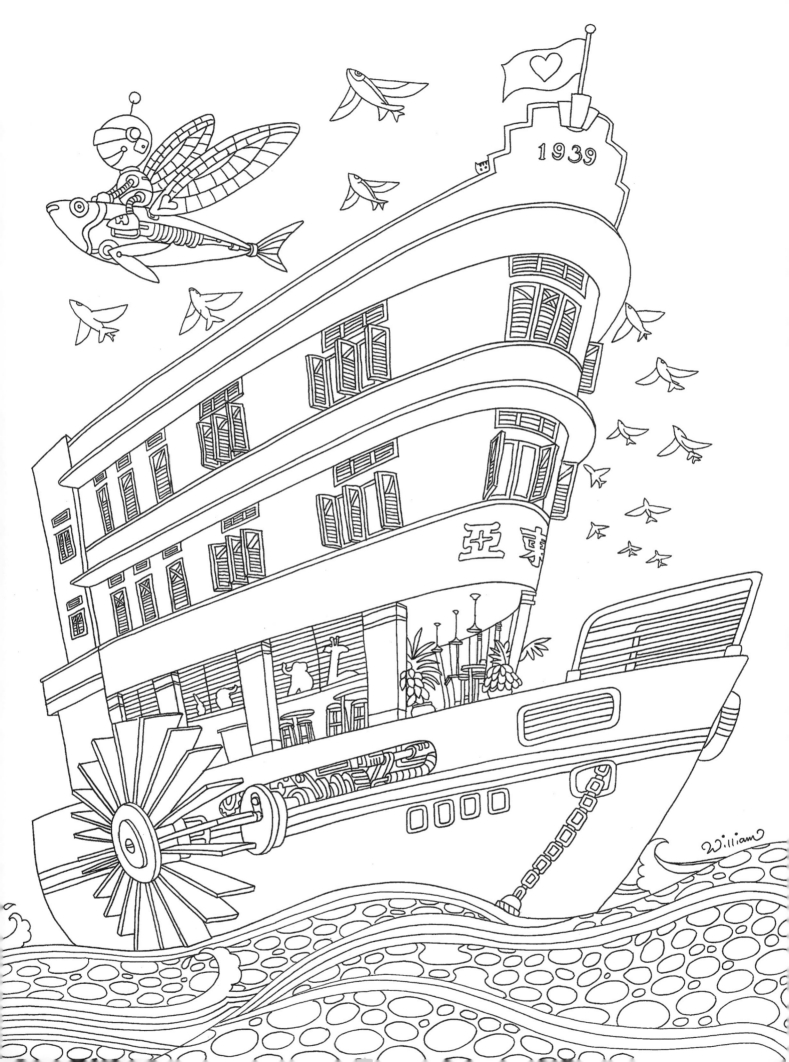

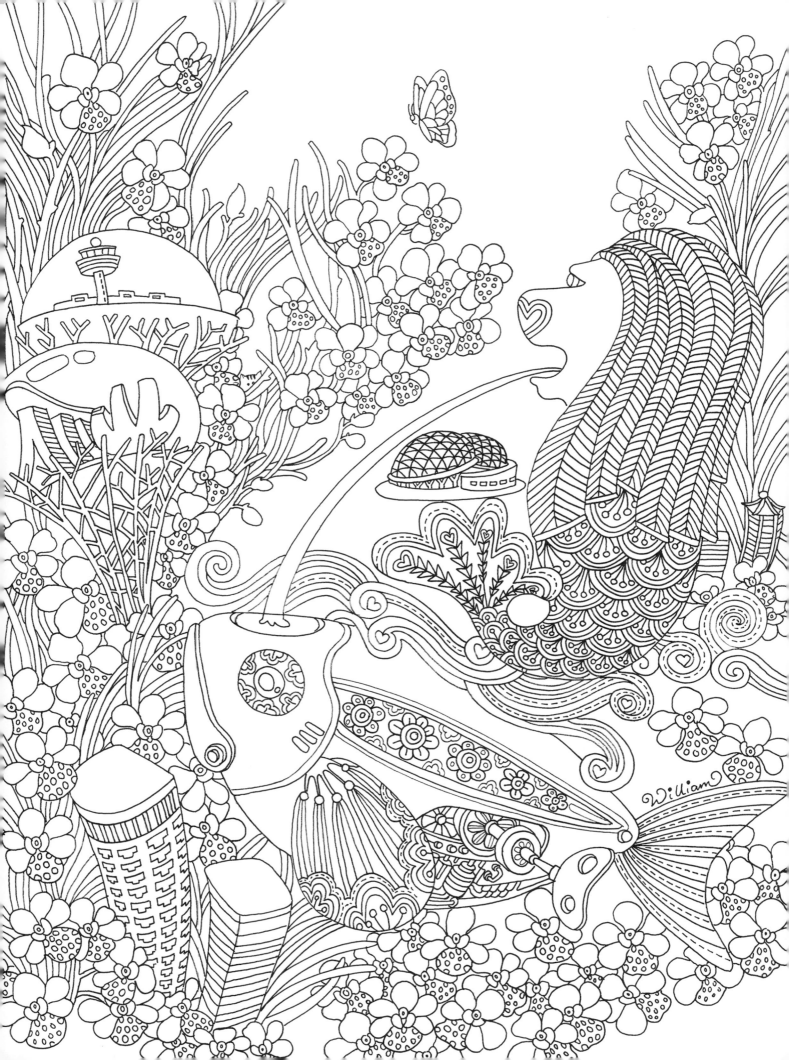

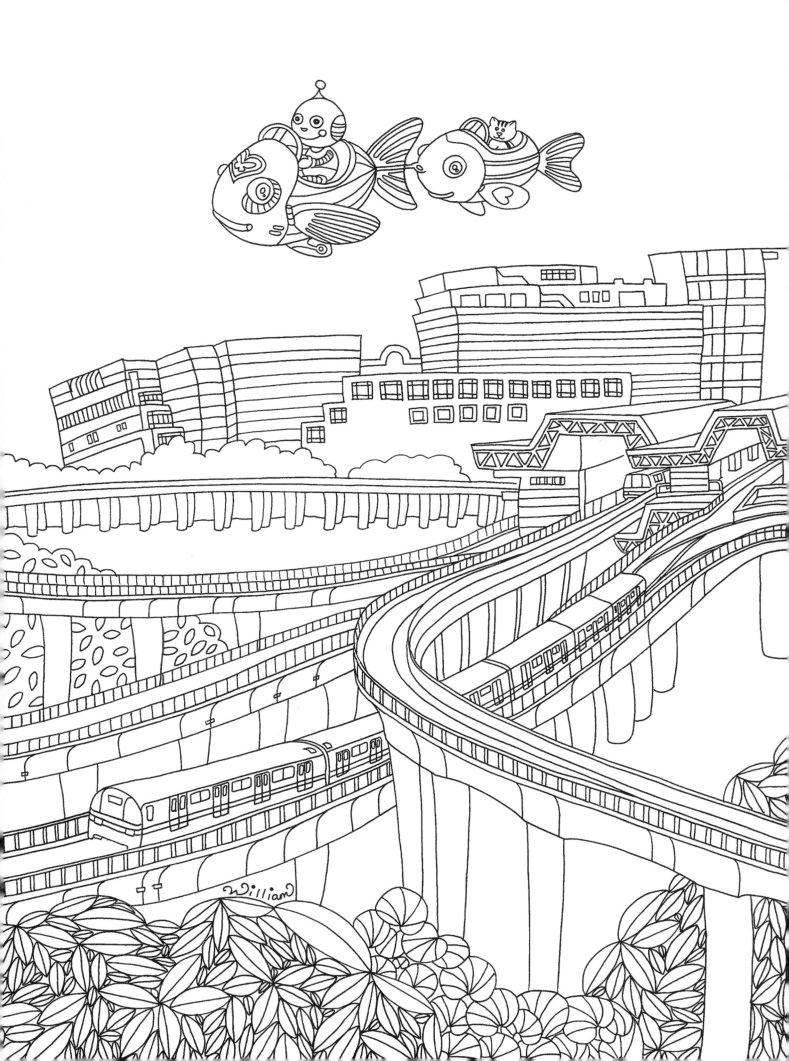

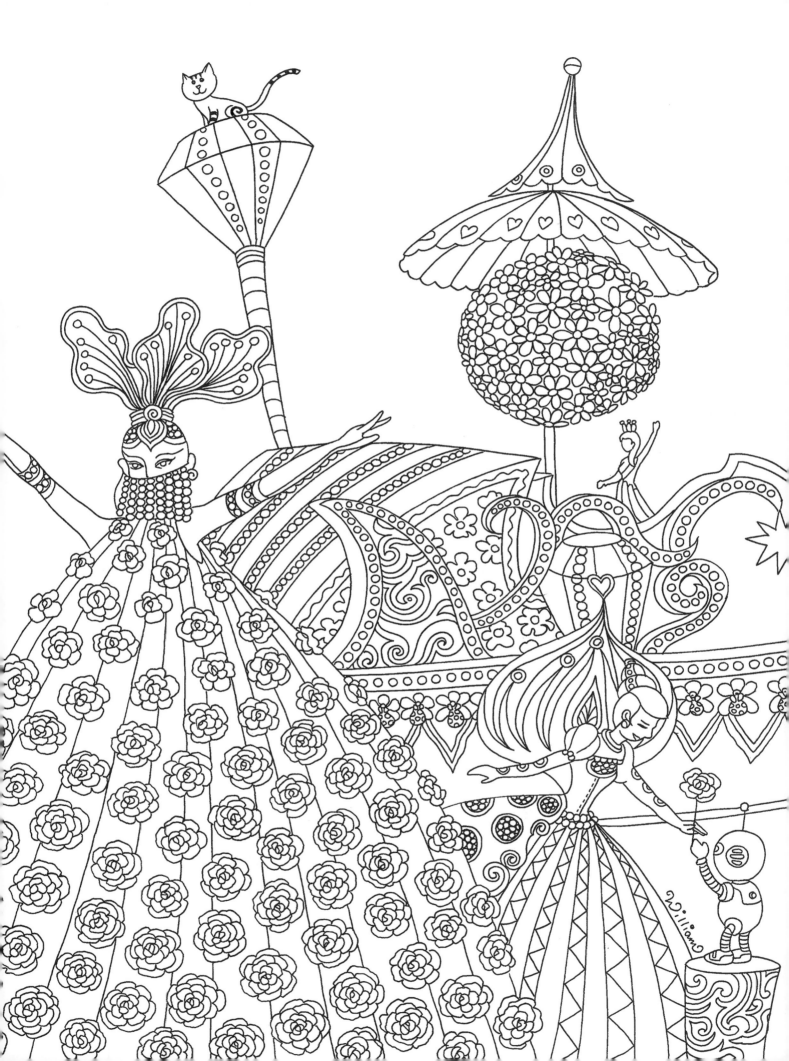

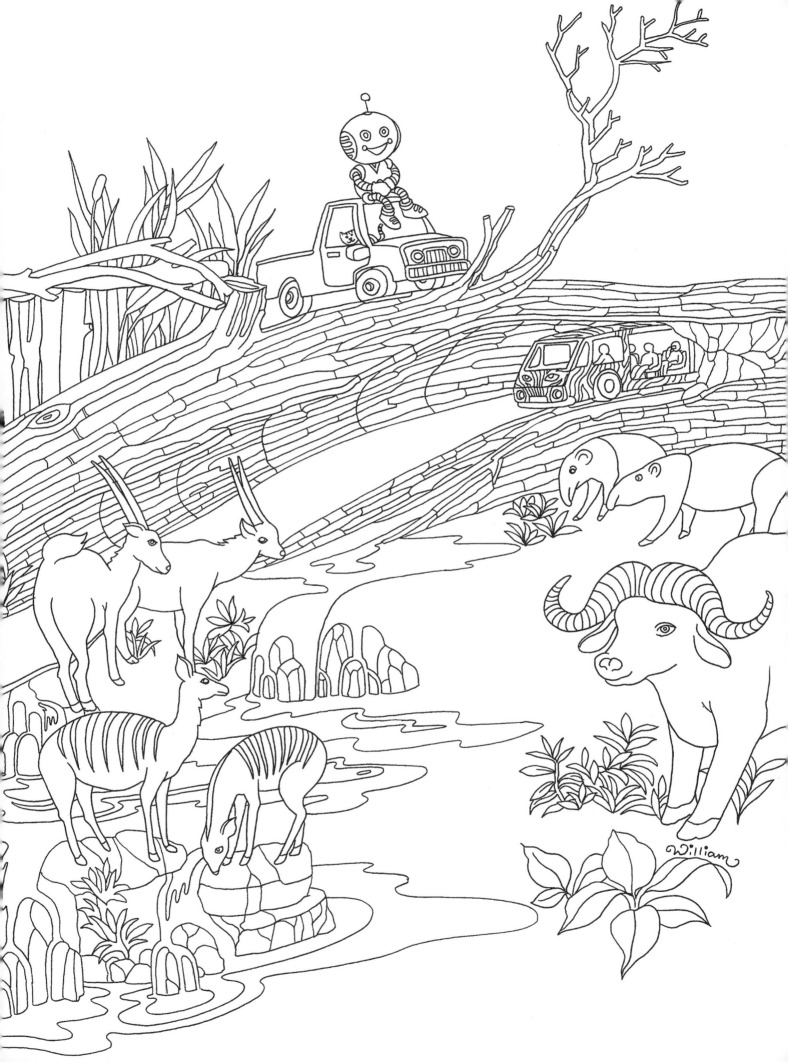

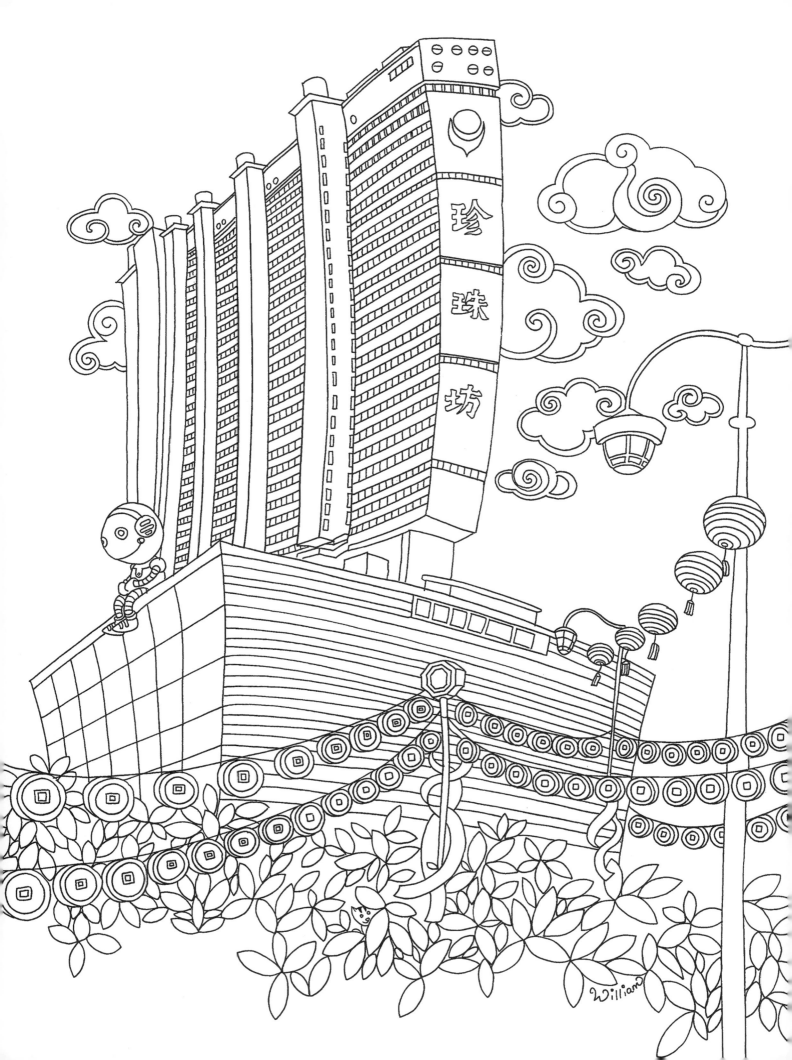

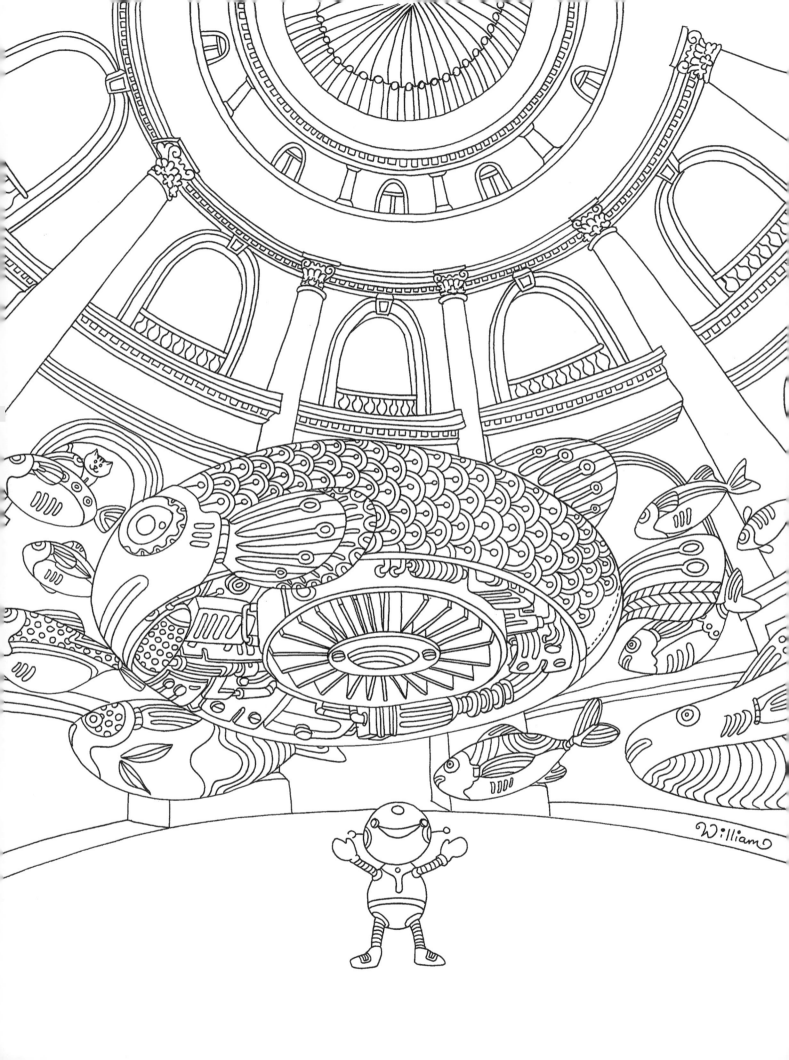

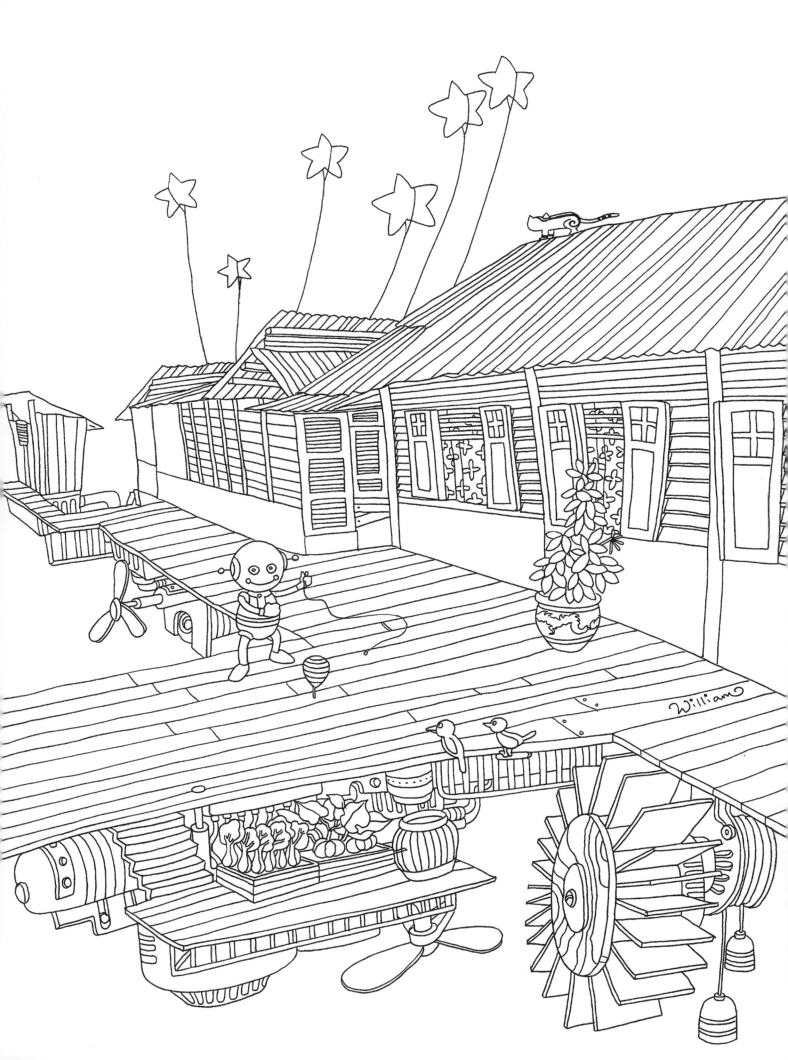

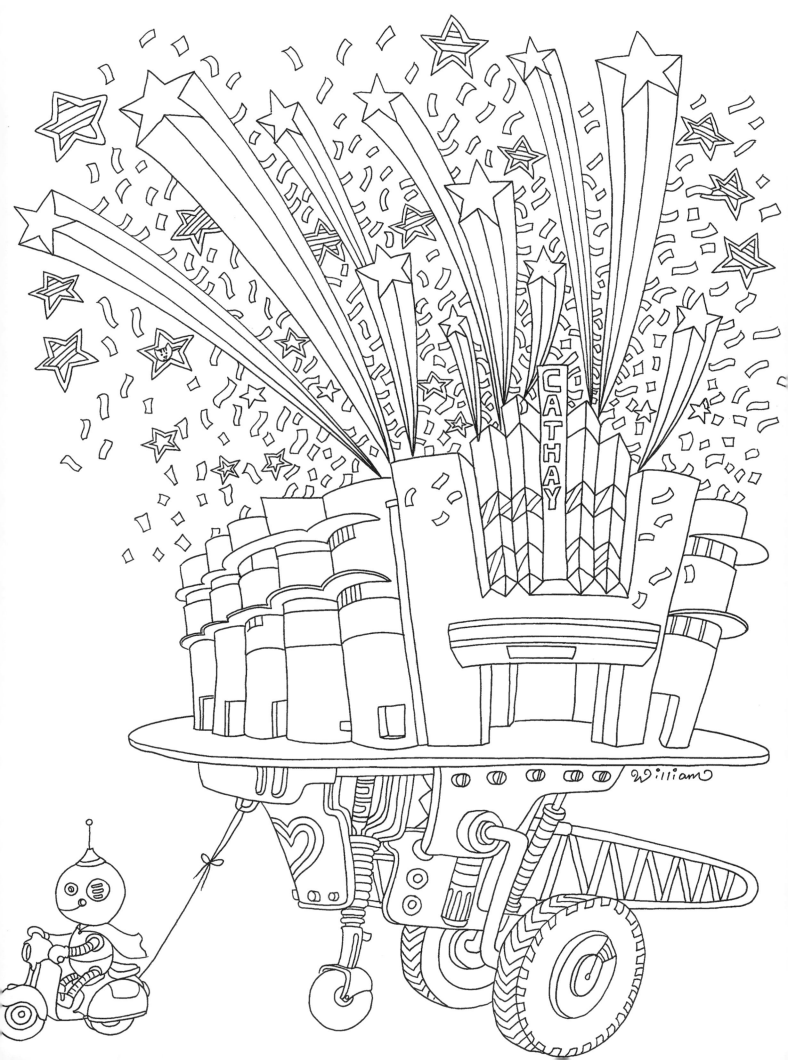

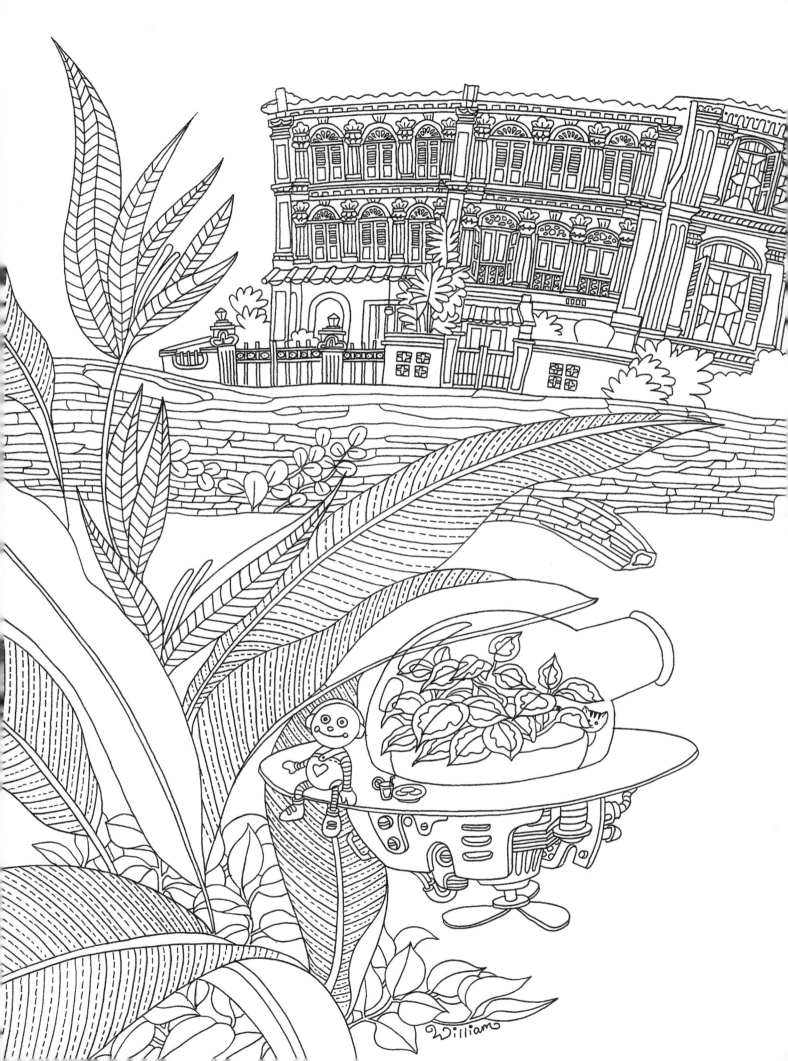

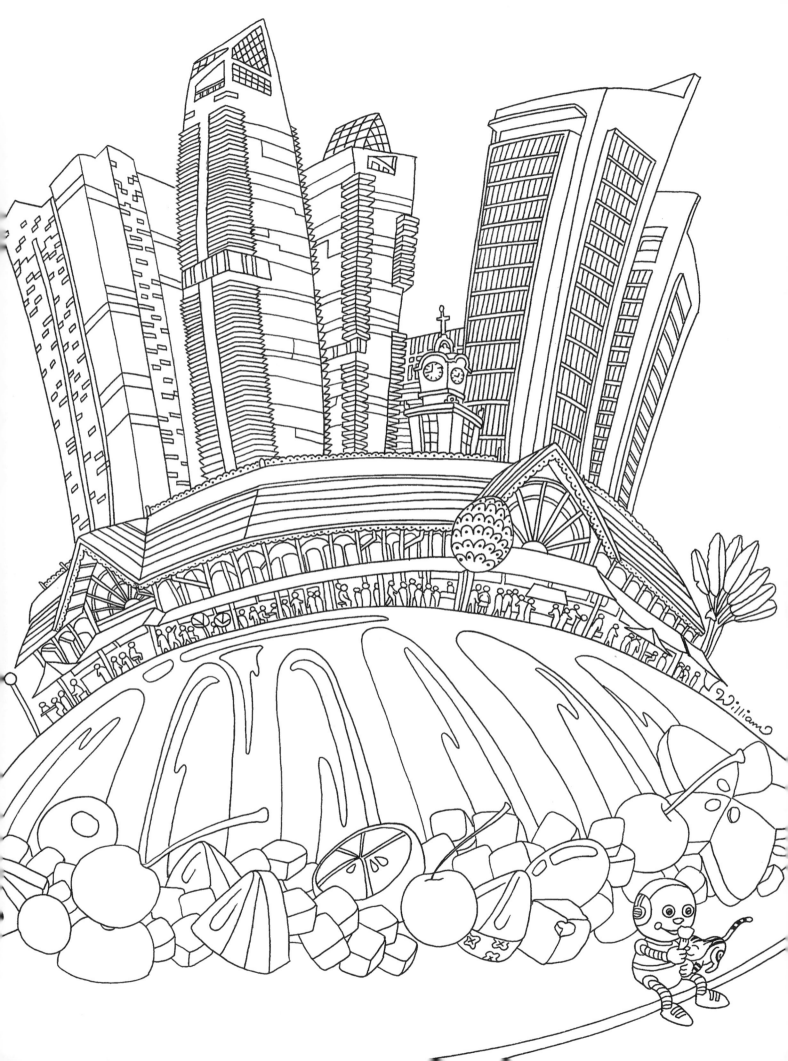

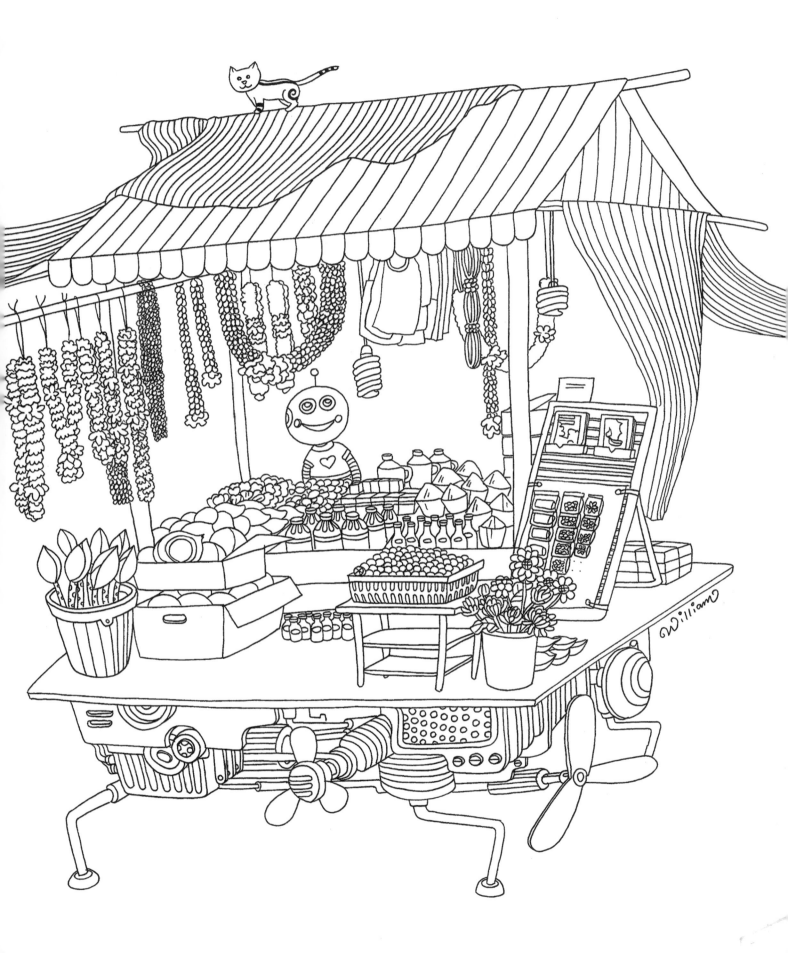

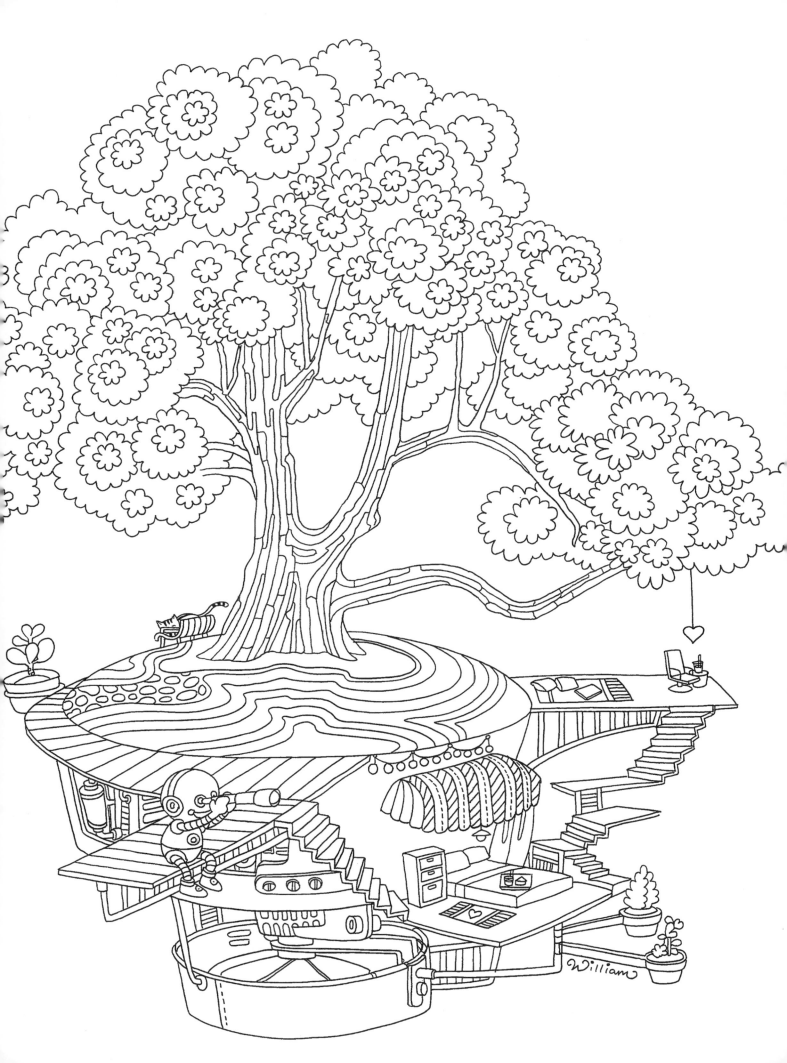

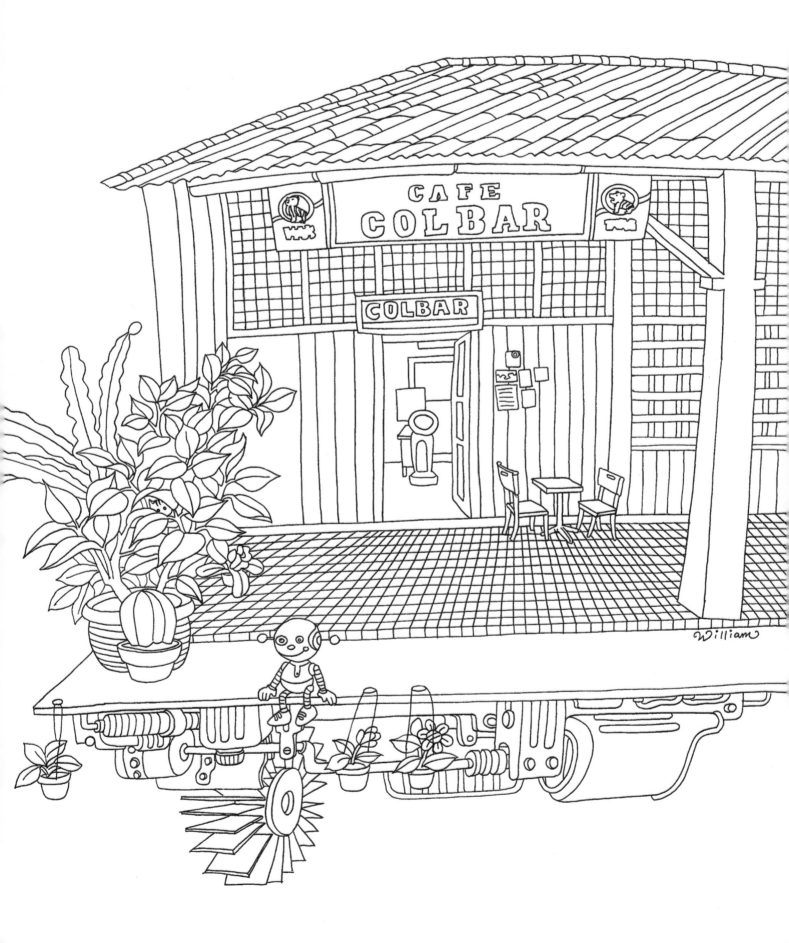

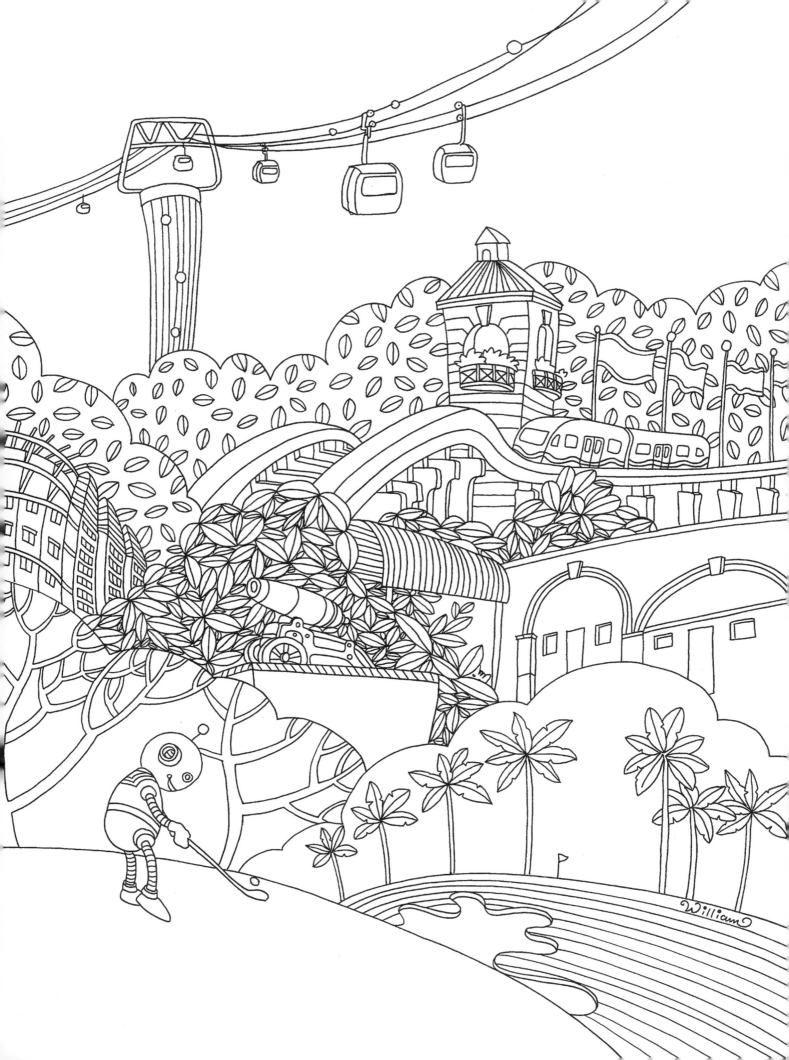

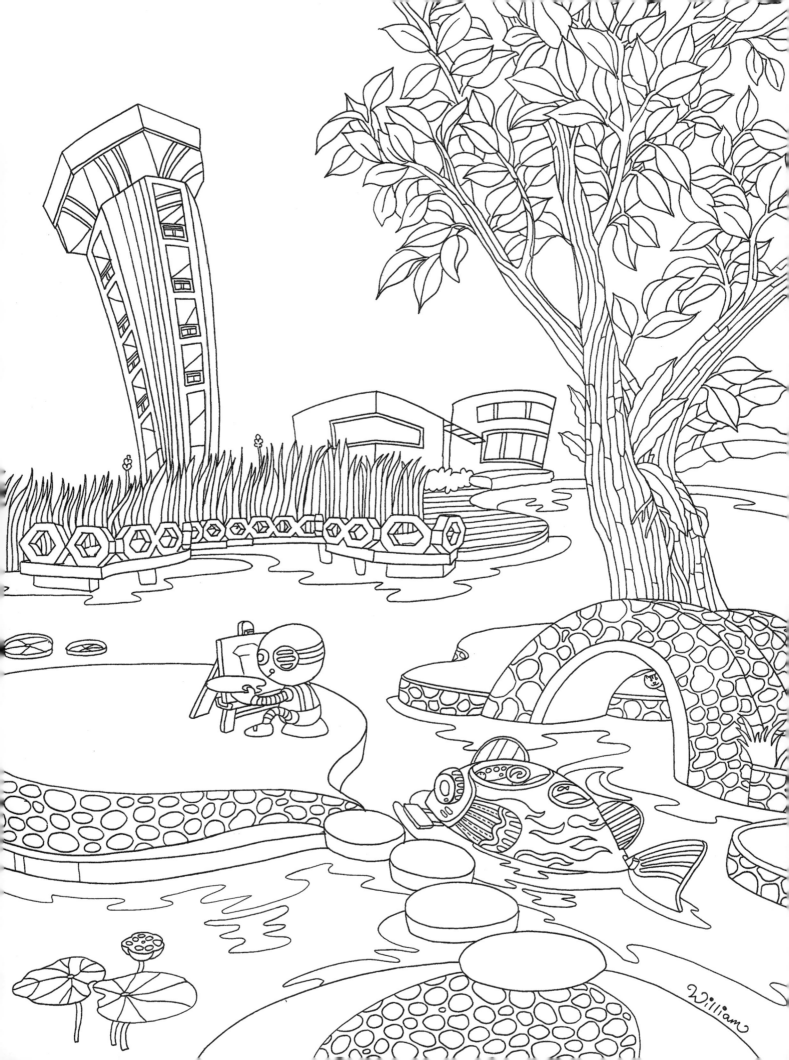

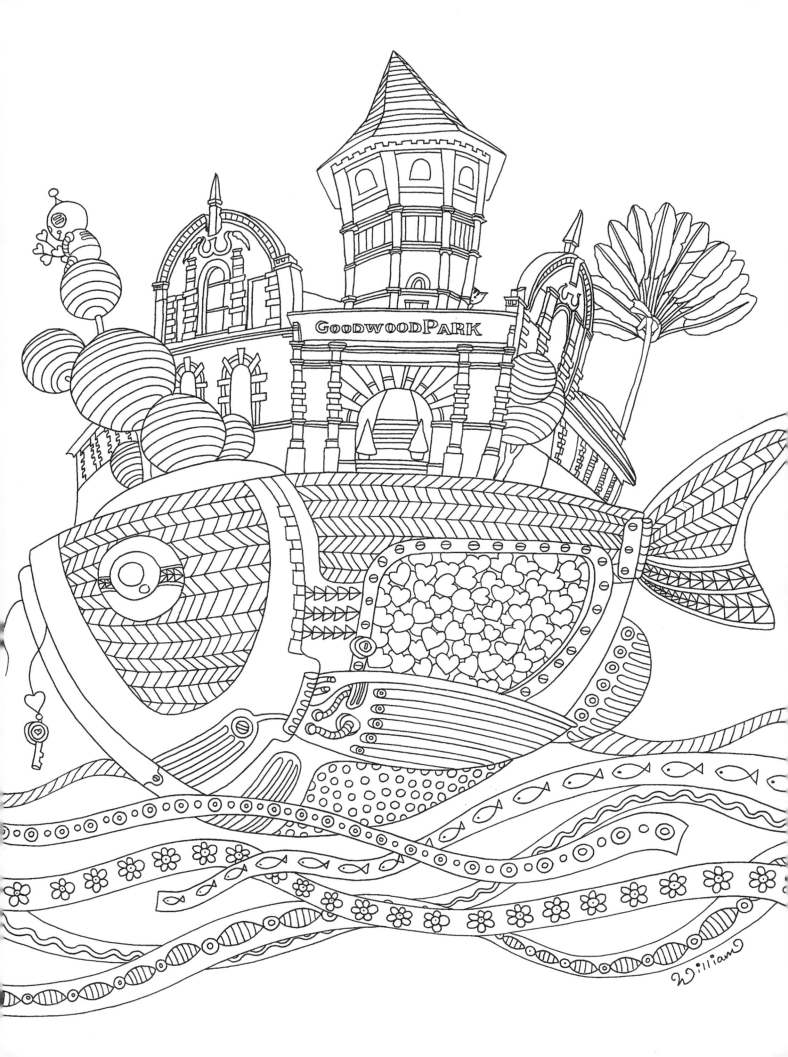

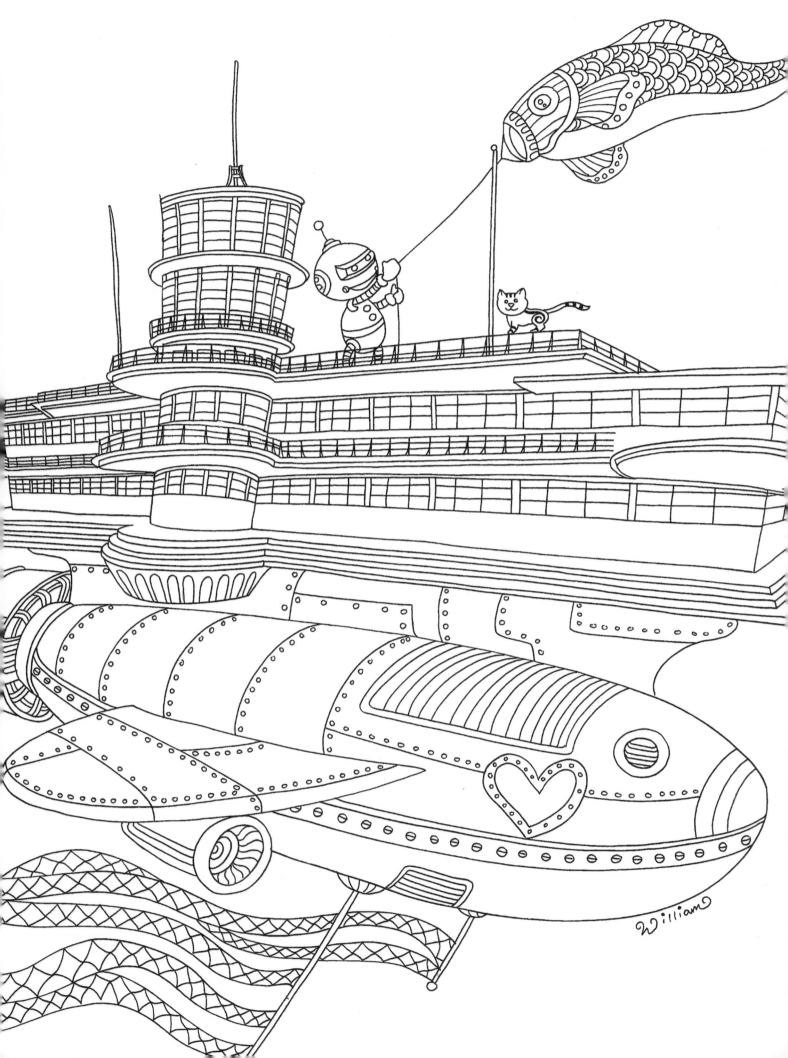

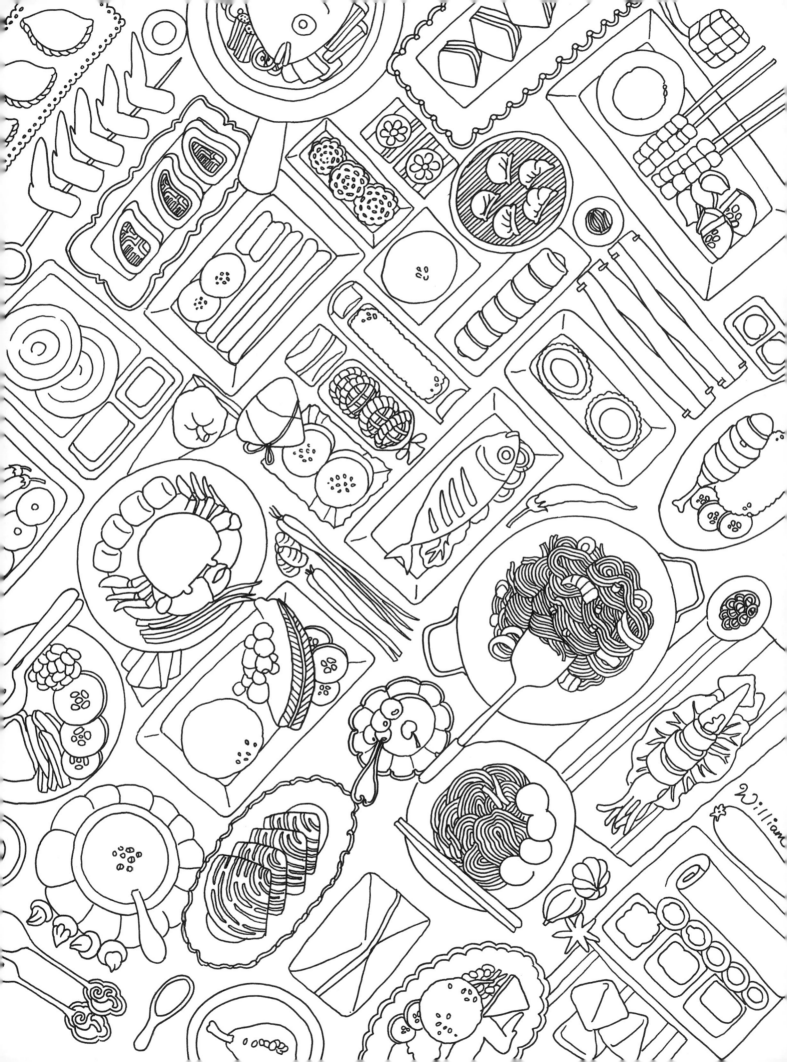